Competing for Quality:

A manager's guide to market testing

by

Lynton Barker

Published by Longman Information and Reference.
Longman Group UK Ltd, 6th Floor,
Westgate House, The High, Harlow Essex CM20 1YR
Telephone: Harlow (0279) 442601; Fax: Harlow (0279) 444501.

A catalogue record for this book is available from the British Library.

ISBN 0−582−23688−6

Printed in Great Britain by
Antony Rowe Ltd, Chippenham, Wiltshire

Acknowledgement

This book is based upon the practical experience of Coopers & Lybrand in public sector market testing. I would like to thank two of my colleagues in Coopers & Lybrand, Phil Halsall and Mike Goodwin, for their help in finalising the book. Over the past five years, the ideas and development work of other colleagues Andrew Heley, Rom Rubycz, Ken Crossland, Tom Devon, John Adamson, Roger Usher and Kevin Rotherham have played a major role in shaping the book's contents. To each of you, thank you for your support and teamwork.

Contents

Appendices:

Foreword

Conceptually, market testing is a simple process. Write a specification, draw up a list of bidders, choose the best bid and implement the results.

In practice however, the introduction of market testing to a large and complex UK public service is fraught with danger, and all those managers currently involved will testify to the range of difficult issues involved. A disciplined and professional approach is needed if market testing is to be successful.

This book is written with the sole purpose of helping managers to be successful in market testing. It gives the background to market testing and offers step by step guidance to all involved.

It is not intended to be exhaustive in its guidance but does set out to provide a total framework for undertaking the processes involved.

There is other essential reading on this topic. In particular managers should read the excellent guides produced by the Public Competition and Purchasing Unit (PCPU), particularly Guidance Note 34 and its revisions which spell out very clearly the rules and boundaries for public sector market testing. For those involved in IS market testing CCTA have produced a clear and focused set of guidelines which are well worth reading and following.

Needless to say, these sources of guidance and the contents of this book should be regarded as advisory only. Specific decisions on market testing must be taken in context. This means that individual departmental guidance or legal advice should be sought in all market tests. What this book will do is point you to the issues and advise you how to go about resolving them.

Best of luck.

Lynton Barker
September 1993

1 Setting the scene

The Government's market testing programme is the means by which public service activity in Britain is being opened up to competition from the private sector. Many refer to it as contracting out but market testing differs in one important way – in-house staff can submit their own tender to try to keep their jobs. As a consequence, the public and private sectors will be bidding against each other for what is estimated to be upwards of £25bn worth of business.

What we are seeing therefore is a process which will put public service management to the test to see whether or not its price and quality can match that of the private sector. Government policy statements such as the Citizen's Charter and the Competing for Quality White Paper have predicted that competition will improve quality and reduce costs.

Will market testing actually achieve this? There have, over many years, already been a number of financial and management initiatives in the public sector. It would be all too easy to dismiss market testing as just another of these; as something which will quickly run its course, be driven into the sands and be forgotten. Judging from its impact, it already seems unlikely that market testing will disappear. Indeed it is a process which can feed on itself and grow rapidly.

How, then, does market testing actually differ from other initiatives? It differs by throwing open to private sector competition the very heartland of the public sector. It allows and encourages the private sector into areas which for many decades have been seen as totally sacrosanct public sector domains, unchallenged and indeed hitherto unchallengeable.

It will not simply be a case of tendering what might be termed marginal public sector activities such as cleaning, catering, guarding and the like, but rather focusing upon what are professional functions 'nearer to the heart of Government'. Market testing seeks to get more, for the same, or less, cost by giving the private sector the chance to involve itself in the operational delivery of major chunks of public service – that is assuming it can prove itself more competent than current public service managers and staff.

By its very nature, market testing represents the biggest challenge and most serious threat yet to the public sector and is seen by many as a form of gradual privatisation. Regardless of where we all stand in terms of our conceptions of the public sector, the potential demise of that body as we currently know it will be viewed with concern, even by many people outside it. It does represent a bastion of democracy, a model of best practice for others to see, and indeed copy.

As the market testing programme develops, the public will be looking for some assurances that the initiative was justified in the first place, and which will more than compensate for the changes which will inevitably occur. Improved quality and reduced costs are implicit in the generic programme. Can market testing deliver these improvements?

Under the market testing process described in detail later in this book, reduced cost (at least initially) is an almost guaranteed outcome. However, reduced cost does not mean better value for money. A fuller picture taking into account costs, quality and security must be viewed before value for money can be determined. A rigorous approach to market testing can deliver these wider benefits. Lets look at the ways in which this might occur.

Questioning of existing service levels

The process of market testing will require a thorough examination of existing services. In doing this a number of fundamental questions will be raised and asked:

- do we need the service at all?

- are there parts of the service which we do not need?

- does the current service provide what the customer wants?

By answering these questions Departments will quantify this and ultimately decide if service activity should be increased (at potential greater cost) or more likely, reduced (to save cost).

Organisational advantages

The bidding and tendering processes involved in market testing will inevitably force public service managers and management to look hard at what they do, how they do it and why they do it. Market testing in local government has sharpened organisational arrangements considerably and resulted in many areas of duplication being removed. It can do the same in Central Government.

Healthy challenges to traditional work practices

It can only be advantageous for any organisation to be forced to examine, in a serious way, how it does its job, and whether it could improve its performance. Such an examination is more meaningful when:

- the continued existence of the organisation is at stake;

- the examiners are external;

- the 'pass or fail' test is no longer one of a relative performance but one of the very best open competition can provide; and

- if different, commercial, innovative approaches can be expected.

Opportunities for innovation

The spirit of innovation to which market testing lends itself will rapidly blow away a good many organisational cobwebs. There will undoubtedly be many instances where the element of competition will bring forth better, and more cost effective, ways of carrying out traditional activities. This is not a direct criticism of the public sector, per se, but will occur naturally in any innovative process, whether public sector or commercial.

Chances for improvements in management

As with the challenges to traditional work practices touched upon above, an examination of a long established organisation will undoubtedly reveal possibilities of substantial and wide ranging management improvements, particularly where public sector constraints do not necessarily have to remain in force.

Dismantling of bureaucracy

The public sector, rightly or wrongly, is closely associated in the public's mind with the establishment of layers of bureaucracy. The market testing process, focusing as it does on value for money and competition, is the ideal tool to uncover and root out examples of overt bureaucracy.

The enabling circumstances

Market testing has been introduced to the public sector by two separate but inter-linked initiatives. The first of these is the Citizen's Charter.

Published in July 1991, the Citizen's Charter, in a section covering 'Delivering Quality', had the following to say:

> *During the 1980's many private companies decided to concentrate on their core businesses and to buy-in services in which they had no particular expertise from specialist contractors. The advantages of this approach apply at least as much in the public sector. It helps to:*
>
> * *set standards – buying-in forces managers to specify measurable standards of the quality of service required, often for the first time;*
>
> * *monitor standards – once standards of service are specified, consumers can check that what is paid for is properly delivered; and*
>
> * *ensure standards are met – the work can be re-done if necessary at no cost to the consumer.*

Secondly, the 'Competing for Quality' White Paper.

The White Paper referred to was published in November 1991. Chapter 1, entitled 'Buying Better Services' says:

> *The Citizen's Charter sets out a comprehensive programme to improve the quality of public services. Central to this programme is the setting of rigorous standards for each service, and the development of ever better methods of delivering those standards. Where the Government takes the citizen's money through taxation, and buys services on the citizen's behalf, there is a heavy obligation to ensure that the services provide the highest quality and the best value that can be bought with that money.*
>
> *Competition is the best guarantee of quality and value for money. In the 1980s, the Government's policy of increasing competition gave a new dynamism to the British economy. We mean to extend those policies in the 1990s. We will expand the frontiers of competition outwards, bringing new benefits to all those who use or work in*

public services. Activities closer to the heart of government will be market tested.

In recent years, private sector businesses have increasingly chosen to concentrate on their core business. They stick with what they know best. And they buy-in specialist contractors to provide new ideas, more flexibility, and a higher level of expertise than could exist in a purely in-house operation. Public sector bodies are increasingly doing the same.

This pressure to market test public service activity is now manifesting itself in substantial programmes throughout government. The process is already producing many complex management issues and will continue to do so. This book seeks to explain what market testing is and how it works, explores the major issues in some depth, identifies and advises on common problems and provides guidelines and checklists for managers, to help them through each stage of the process.

2 Introducing the process

When can market testing be applied?

Before describing the process of market testing, how do managers
know whether their particular business can be market tested? What
are the essential determinants?

There are two crucial factors:

- firstly, it must be possible to specify with sufficient clarity what is
  wanted. In simple terms, if there is no identifiable end product,
  then there can be no legal contract and the market testing process
  cannot be applied;

- secondly, the purchaser and the provider must be capable of clear
  separation.

This sounds relatively straightforward and indeed, in most commercial applications, it is, since the contractor will normally serve
either one, or a number of, customers or clients, working to a
specified contract or a set of clearly distinguishable relationships.

However, in a number of public service situations, either the
passage of time, or the ad-hoc development of managerial roles has
meant that accountabilities and responsibilities are often unclear.
Managers will have shared, often disparate, functions with clear lines
of demarcation being the exception rather than the rule. Different
parts of the same 'business' are sometimes undertaken by different
groups with different reporting lines, and often differently framed
aims and objectives.

These arrangements tend to reflect history rather than planned and
structured decision making, and as a consequence it is often difficult
to disentangle the threads.

What must exist, however, at an early stage of any market testing
process is a clear and unambiguous separation between the client and
the contractor. The client is responsible for the specification and
monitoring the service: the contractor is responsible for the delivery
to specified standards of that service. Without such a clear-cut

separation, the market testing process will flounder and value for money will sink in muddy waters.

The in-house bidder and separation

To complicate matters, in most instances in the public sector there will be what is called an in-house bidder. This is a bidder from within the current providers organisation. Whenever there is to be an in-house bid, the organisation must create what is called the client role and a separate and distinct in-house contractor role.

If there is no clear separation between the in-house bidder and the present service provider on the one hand, and the market testers and the client on the other, then the signals sent to industry about the robustness and fairness of the competition might well lead to a lower level of competitive response from the market, and accusations of anti-competitive behaviour.

Given the substantial value of potential contracts and the high risk of legal challenges from unsuccessful bidders, (and somebody in each of these companies will be asked why they lost, having spent a great deal of money on the tender process), it may prove increasingly prudent for Departments not only to separate these functions internally, but in some instances to contract-out the market testing process itself.

It is no bad thing to over emphasise the fact that great care must be taken to ensure fairness and even-handedness as between the in-house bidders and other external bidders at all stages. This subject is touched upon at various points in the book.

What is the market testing process?

How does the process of market testing actually work? There are in fact six distinct phases to the process. Each phase is dealt with in its own right and at greater length in subsequent chapters. The purpose of this chapter is to provide a very broad based, over-arching view of the totality of the process, so that as readers move through the book they have a reference point at which they can identify what is to come and where each phase fits in with the others.

Lets look briefly then at the various phases.

Phase 1 – getting started

Here, right at the outset of the process, all that will have been determined is a very broad programme determining which parts of the Department will be subject to market testing, and which general timescales might be involved. The thrust behind the establishment of the programme may be no more than a firm commitment by Ministers that an agreed percentage of a Department will be subject to market testing in year one, perhaps a further percentage in year two and so forth.

What needs to be done is to set up the machinery which will run the market testing process in the most efficient and effective way to deal with all strategic and operational aspects of market testing over several years.

The oversight and control of the process will fall, in normal circumstances, to a Steering Group. This will generally comprise senior managers with the necessary interest and expertise. The Steering Group will have specific terms of reference and clearly designated responsibilities. It should be sufficiently senior to be able to reach decisions quickly and informally, but not too large as to become cumbersome in decision-taking.

In addition, market testing teams will need to pick up the projects. Expertise and experience will be at a premium. If such teams do not already exist within the Department, training will be necessary. The size and complexity of a typical Government Department market testing programme will mean that the creation of several market testing teams, usually supported and advised by a central market testing unit, will be the most practical way to operate. This means that a market testing unit can stay in existence over many market tests. In contrast, a specific market test team can supervise perhaps one or two market tests, and then cease to exist.

Whilst the actual management structure is bound to vary from one organisation to another, a typical framework structure and roles are shown in the chart in Figure 2.1.

Even at this early stage, thought needs to be given to the organisation known as the client side, which will have the eventual responsibilities of overseeing and monitoring the contract once it has been let. Eventually, the market testing team will need to consider and make recommendations on the organisation, structure, tasks, responsibilities and accountabilities of the client side, as well as ensuring that sufficient resources have been set aside for it at the appropriate time. Organisations vary in size and complexity and therefore this frame-

9

Figure 2.1

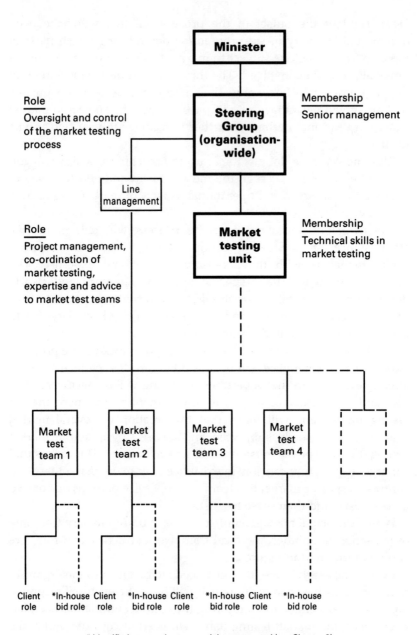

Role

Oversight and control
of the market testing
process

Membership

Senior management

Role

Project management,
co-ordination of
market testing,
expertise and advice
to market test teams

Membership

Technical skills in
market testing

* Identified at an early stage and then separated (see Chapter 3)

work will not fit all situations precisely. The basic principles to follow are:

- a person or group should take on overall responsibility (see example of Steering Group);

- a person or a team should direct specific market tests (see example of market testing team);

- there should be a source of specialist advisers and support (see the example of market testing unit).

Flowing from this, an action plan will need to be drawn up, linked into the timescale, identifying the stages to be gone through, and their cut off dates. This plan will also allocate tasks and responsibilities connected with the process. It will cover such areas as management arrangements, objectives and estimated resource requirements.

One other important function needs to be carried out at this stage – the initial briefing and the establishment of on-going formal consultation arrangements for the TUS and for those staff members likely to be affected by the market testing process.

Phase 2 – detailed planning

This phase sees a 'focusing down' from the necessarily broadly based over-all programme approved by Ministers, to the more specific activities or combinations of activities which will actually come under the market testing microscope. Two separate aspects come into play here. First, from an internal view point, which activities or groups of activities fit well together and would make a reasonable package? Internal politics are inevitably bound to play a significant part here, and the Steering Group, who will have a clear role to play, will need to take a firm and unbiased view of the Department's interests at this stage. The second aspect must be a commercial one, slightly more difficult at this stage. The eventual packages for presentation to industry must have the necessary attraction to potential bidders.

A vital aspect at this point is the preparation of a business analysis. This, properly done, will provide the Department with the necessary financial and other information to enable them to make the best decisions in terms of packaging, once they have the necessary 'feel' for the market. A report through the Steering Group, outlining the best packaging options, together with the advantages and disadvantages of each, will normally form the basis of the eventual decision as to which option to go for.

This phase also sees the identification and selection of any potential in-house bid team, with, most importantly, a named leader. It may of course be necessary to change the team structure once the actual scope of the market test is known, but it is none the less important to have a team planned at this early stage and to begin to address the question of conflicts of interest.

Phase 3 – specifications and tender strategy

The most important aspect of this phase is to arrive at a specification of the business being market tested, which will not only encapsulate the essence and practicalities of the business, but will allow maximum flexibility and opportunity for innovation to the bidders. Different businesses will call for different levels of specification, and the chapter which develops this point (Chapter 5) clearly spells out the work involved in this phase.

This phase also sees the initial identification of potential bidders from the market place, to take part in the open competition. Here again, it is vital to have the ability to attract the right sort of potential bidders. A very informed understanding of the market and the competition is a vital part of this process. Intelligent procurement relies on an understanding of the market place and what can be achieved in terms of value for money. Buying services is not like buying tins of beans. This phase will also see the finalisation of the overall contract strategy, which will eventually be 'signed off' by the Steering Group. It will encompass decisions as to the type of contract, the timescale envisaged and the list of selected bidders.

At the same time, the Steering Group will need to decide upon the size, shape and structure of the client organisation which will be put in place once the contract has been let – this client organisation having the responsibility for the eventual monitoring and management of the contract.

The in-house team, during this phase, will need to be preparing themselves as thoroughly as they can for the imminent bidding/ tendering phase. Their major task at this point is the preparation of a commercial business model, to assist them in the vital transition from internal to market viability.

Phase 4 – the bidding process

During this phase bidders will be preparing and putting forward their bids for the contracts. This includes the in-house bidders, and before the eventual deadline set for the receipt of bids there will be an on-going series of discussions and briefings controlled by the market testing team. These will involve, perhaps at different points, all the various parties, and will be aimed at the clarification of issues and final establishment of parameters and flexbilities. Care must of course, be taken to treat all tenderers fairly and equitably.

Once the bids are in, a tender evaluation panel will evaluate them in accordance with already established (and published) criteria and, ideally, an evaluation model. The eventual recommendation from the tender evaluation panel is submitted with a full report to the Steering Group for final approval. In some instances, post tender negotiations will take place where suggestions for adjustments (not just of price!), by either party, might be made to improve value for money. Again, commercial confidentiality and the elements of fairness must be strictly observed.

Once a decision is final, the proposed client organisation will also need to be made aware that a decision has been reached, and will take over the final letting processes and the monitoring/management of the contract. Plans will need to have been prepared to deal with unsuccessful bidders, staff and TUS, dependent upon the range of outcomes.

Phase 5 – implementing the results

Probably the most pressing and immediate task in the implementation phase will be to inform the unsuccessful bidders of the outcome. All bidders, successful or not, will have invested a good deal of resources and money in the preparation and presentation of their bids. In the event of failure to win the contract they will need to justify, commercially, the expenditure of these resources, and to some extent their own judgments are 'on the line'. A constructive and helpful approach to debriefing unsuccessful bidders, including perhaps such things as an indication of what were seen as weaknesses in the bid, is essential.

As for the successful contractor, any negotiated amendments to the contract (e.g. post-tender negotiation alterations) will need to be taken on board, and the Department for its part, needs to ensure that all its contractual obligations have been fulfilled.

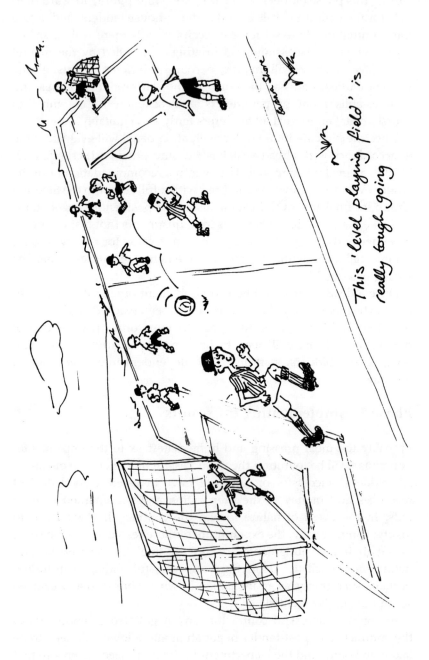

If the in-house bidder has been successful, a slightly different approach will be called for in terms of ensuring a soundly based and smooth transition from a non-commercial to a commercial environment. Some training, familiarisation and adaptation will be necessary.

It will be at this stage that extremely careful handling of TUS/staff relations will be of great importance, and specialist/legal advice will often be needed.

The client organisation will be formally activated during this phase, and will initially need to take great care in managing the contract, since unsuccessful bidders will be watching closely and will be quick to pick up any variations or non-compliance. Formal and specific training of the client organisation members will play an important part in the eventual smooth running of the contract.

It will be most important to forge links and to establish trust between the client organisation and the contractors (internal or external) at an early stage.

Phase 6 – ongoing contract management

The client organisation's responsibility in this phase consists primarily of monitoring and managing the contract properly – that is, ensuring contract compliance with no fall in service levels or quality or, if the market or customer requirements call for any variations, to see that these variations are properly carried out and managed. This is a vital aspect, given that the previous unsuccessful bidders will still be waiting in the wings, ready to call foul at any stage. The client organisation will need to be pro-active in terms of market/customer awareness rather than re-active.

Further down the line lies the aspect of another competition. The client organisation will have to plan well ahead for this, and take on board any relevant considerations in terms of contract extension.

At the end of the contract period, there is, of course, the decision, using the experience of the current contract as a guide, as to whether the contract as it stands should be re-let, whether the boundaries should be extended, or indeed whether the present business would be re-let in a different way.

The six phases of market testing are illustrated in Figure 2.2.

Strategic issues

This then paints a broadly based picture of the market testing process as a whole, and succeeding chapters illustrate the various separate

Figure 2.2 The six phases of market testing

	PHASE 1 Getting started	PHASE 2 Detailed planning	PHASE 3 Specifications & tender strategy	PHASE 4 The bidding process	PHASE 5 Implementing the results	PHASE 6 Ongoing contract management
Client side activity	Set up management machinery. Make appointments to key groups. Establish outline programmes. Establish policy ground rules. Prepare action plans.	Evaluate proposed activities in more detail. Develop outline tender strategy. Provide training for key staff. Begin market analysis. Select best options for market testing. Get clearance on market test programme and outline tender strategy.	Prepare service specifications and contract documents. Continue to clarify policy ground rules. Identify potential bidders. Identify evaluation criteria. Finalise contract strategy.	Commence formal tendering process. Bidding processes and presentation of bids. Tender evaluation. Post tender negotiations. Detailed evaluation report.	Communicate results. Debrief. Establish future organisation and formalise links. Ensure contract compliance. Introduce contract regime.	Continue contract compliance. Maintain awareness of customer and market. Prepare for next competition.
In-house bid team activity		Identify in-house team. Formulate in-house team strategy.	In-house team review and analysis. Development of in house business plan.	Develop bid strategy. Submit in-house bid.	Mobilise in-house service if successful. Establish client and contractor working systems.	Manage in-house service to budget. Continue to improve performance in readiness for next competition.

→ emerging client/contractor split →

CLIENT/CONTRACTOR SPLIT IN PLACE

phases in considerably more detail. It would be worth while before moving on to such technical detail, however, to pause for a moment and expose a number of important strategic issues which occur frequently during the market testing process. A knowledge that they exist, or could occur, will better inform managers in their approach to their own market testing processes.

One of the major considerations stems from the potential involvement of public servants – certainly during the initial phases and conceivably during the contract phases – in a process which exposes them, both personally and in career terms, to a threatening culture shock. Let's look at this more closely.

The people involved

The descriptions of market testing processes tend to refer to organisations, teams or groups. However, it is important not to lose sight of the fact that what is actually being talked about are people – people with their own thoughts, hopes, expectations, dreams and fears.

In the public sector, people have been schooled, often over many years, in the public sector culture. What does this mean in practical terms? In the public sector, the collegiate approach is paramount – decisions are taken in a gradual way, and often over an extended period of time, against the background of a 'safe' atmosphere. In general, as the civil servant is reluctant to take risks, the inability to manage risks is built into the system.

In sharp contrast, let us take a quick look at the world which is promised by the market testing process. This world is contract driven not culture driven – risk is an everyday occurrence and there is an in-built necessity to face and to manage risk. Furthermore, failure has also to be managed – indeed in general the market learns from failure and becomes better and more competitive because of it. Advancement is also performance based. There can no longer be in-built expectations of getting on by simply getting by. On the contrary, there is now a positive need to innovate, to deliberately take risks, provided that these have been evaluated and are justifiable.

The focus switches from bureaucracy to service delivery, to the cost/quality continuum – these are new concepts to most public servants. As for career expectations, the work of market testing envisages set contract lengths (some as short as three years). Managers careers are, therefore, on the line at the end of each specific period – there are no more safe havens which can be expected to last throughout one's career. For example, given the normal contract length, there will be a need to win and perform well on, for example, ten different contracts in one career.

In short, then, it is not difficult to see why the threat of market testing might well cause fear, resentment, hostility and resistance in some public servants, and the clear danger is that those feelings may conceivably, and sometimes understandably, spill over into their handling of, and reactions to, the process itself. This, in turn, could well have a negative or detrimental effect upon the validity or effectiveness of that particular market testing process. There is no single or simple answer, but managers should not lose sight of these factors at any stage.

Organisational considerations

Similar changes are envisaged in terms of organisation. In so far as structures are concerned, there will be a clear need for a flatter pyramid. Decisions will need to be taken more quickly, and at different levels. Promotion may be less but possible rewards may be greater. Eventually, payment may well be by results or by performance rather than by grade or by years of service.

One of the most affected areas could be top management – the open structure as it stands today may be fundamentally challenged. Similarly the 'fast stream' could become virtually self selecting in the light of contract results over a period of time.

A total rethink will be called for in terms of personnel, training, postings and recruitment policies. There will be much less need for central controls as business becomes contract driven. Similarly, there will be much less need for policy areas as client/contractor relationships are established throughout the whole of the public sector.

Financial

One of the major organisational rethinks will need to be in the field of finance. Most of the areas under consideration for market testing have hitherto been subject to the constraints of public accounting systems. This in some ways dictates, and possibly slows down, the nature of progress and development in these particular areas. The market testing process lends itself to flexibility and innovation and with the removal of such financial constraints, some wide-ranging financial changes could follow. Specific examples might be the introduction of commercial, financial management systems, the introduction of investment strategy changes, due regard to income flows, and a whole new raft of pricing policies. The introduction or imposition of these different financial regimes will call for important considerations on which commercial view points and experiences are widely different, for obvious reasons, to those in the public sector.

Culture

One of the most important factors within a successful service-orientated company is the recognised and accepted culture of that company. In general terms the cultural values of the better commercial firm are about valued, friendly, innovative and flexible teams whose survival and growth, as a team and as individuals, relies on empowering customers.

This culture is a key element in getting the best out of staff and is, crucially, being perceived as having each customer's best interests at heart. Over time, this will allow an informal and flexible development of a different VFM service being negotiated as client and contractor work together to solve problems.

Most private sector service companies strive for the following cultural values:

- valuing all staff;
- one overall culture;
- flexible;
- enabling;
- supportive;
- encouraging innovation;

- team orientated;
- motivated;
- rewarding;
- decisive;
- accessible;
- trained staff.

Structure

The commercial approach generally, is to select (and probably to recruit specifically) a manager to deliver the service under the contract and within budget. The need for a clear, visible and strong leader with decision making powers managing flexible multiple disciplinary terms is perceived by the better contractors as an essential element in a successful longer term contract.

In brief, the service delivery is assured by an accountable manager, able to measure and reward individuals as well as the team, interfacing with the client side and customers to solve problems and to ensure customer satisfaction. Features of structure in this context are as follows:

- visible, strong leader;

- leadership/direction;

- clear roles;

- understanding of other people's roles;

- delegated responsibility/authority;

- facility for consultation and decisions to be made with expert inputs;

- multi-disciplinary flexible teams.

People issues

The people issues centre around creating greater flexibility in flatter pyramids. The commercial response to an invitation to tender is likely to be based on a highly motivated and positive group of staff who do whatever needs to be done to support the customer. It is a strong possibility that under commercial conditions this pool of staff will be somewhat smaller than the staff doing the job within the public sector.

Similarly, the emphasis is likely to be one of greater responsibility and fewer levels of supervision. In-house teams capable of developing greater flexibility and customer orientation will have more chance of succeeding.

In terms of culture and people, these issues are perhaps not as far removed from current public sector scenarios as might be expected. Clearly, management needs to be sharper, better informed and more focused, and perhaps different levels of commitment might be called for from staff, but the differences in overall terms are perhaps not as great, or as insurmountable, as might at first be imagined or feared.

Two other points, public procurement law and TUPE, are worthy of mention in their own right.

Public procurement law

There are two aspects of procurement law which must be borne in mind for each market test.

Firstly, there now exists a set of EC procurement rules which must be observed if the market test activity falls within the definition of activities covered by EC GATT. Market testing activities are caught where the procurement rules cover advertising, times for responses, market pre-qualification and tender evaluation.

Secondly, contractors who believe that procurement processes have been manipulated to their disadvantage or conducted outside EC GATT rules can bring actions either through national court or the EC courts.

In order to guide managers on this subject a summary of procurement law is included in Appendix 5.

Beyond this your own procurement advisers will be able to guide you.

The implications of TUPE

Market testing raises a number of personnel issues whose recognition and treatment by Departments may have a significant impact on both the well being of individual members of staff and the continuity of the service. Staff will be faced with uncertainty over their future and will be looking for answers to a number of questions; – will they have to work in the private sector, if so will their terms and conditions be the same as they are now, or indeed will they have a job at all when the market test is completed?

Continuing uncertainty of this nature is not only of concern to the employees but must also be a concern to Departments – concern that a viable service will be maintained until the market test is completed. Service quality may gradually degrade as competent staff seek and obtain employment elsewhere; even worse, the service might be severely disrupted through the malicious action of disgruntled employees.

The ultimate impact on staff, when measured in terms of preserving employment and existing terms and conditions, will depend on whether the Transfer of Undertakings, (Protection of Employment) Regulations 1981 (TUPE) applies to the market test.

It is now well known by all managers and staff affected by market testing that where TUPE does apply, employees can expect their

existing terms and conditions (excluding pensions) to transfer intact to the outsourcing supplier as of day one.

However, there is still a considerable degree of uncertainty over this matter and senior managers, staff unions and lawyers are predicting a barrage of legal challenges which, it is claimed, will generate the necessary case law to provide effective guidance for market testing. In the meantime, senior managers must deal with this issue in a cautious and sensible manner.

At time of writing, government Departments are taking the line that contractors must decide whether or not TUPE will apply and reflect their judgement on this issue in their bids. Without substantial case law this appears to be a sensible course of action.

The best advice for senior managers at the time of publication of this book is to be aware of TUPE, do not underestimate its potential impact on market testing, read the more detailed notes in Appendix 6 of this book and consult your own legal advisers and legal Department on the implications for individual market tests.

Where TUPE applies, private sector suppliers seemingly have less scope to reduce costs by employing fewer staff or offering more modest terms and conditions, and their success in the market test may well depend then on their ability to utilise the existing staff more effectively, i.e. by using them on work other than that for the Department. Large IT suppliers, by virtue of their sheer size and the range of skills they employ, are likely to be able to meet this challenge.

Regardless of the policy framework which eventually emerges there are steps which should be taken to reduce staff uncertainties and provide a better environment in which to manage the service through the market testing programme. In particular:

(a) assess the likely applicability of TUPE: the likely form of each market test package should be tested against the TUPE criteria (issued to all government departments by the Cabinet Office, to establish whether it is likely to apply);

(b) establish the staff implications: for each of the test packages, identify the likely outcomes and the number of staff who are likely to be surplus to requirements;

(c) evaluate Departmental transfer options: assess, by grade, skill and age group, the possibility to staff transfers to other parts of the Department;

(d) evaluate external transfer options: enter into further informal dialogue with potential suppliers to assess their ability to absorb staff (over and above the number they assess to be necessary to carry out the work). Such an approach would have to be made cautiously, recognising that providing the supplier with much detail on staff skills and competence could seriously prejudice an in-house bid;

(e) prepare a voluntary/early retirement package: depending on the outcome of (c) and (d) above prepare an attractive package, e.g. incorporating retraining/career counselling benefits, and seek volunteers for the package;

(f) cost the likely outcomes: based on (c), (d) and (e) assess whether non TUPE compliant bids at different cost levels are likely to be attractive and establish the likely redundancy costs associated with all of the scenarios and assess the funding implications;

(g) consult TUS and communicate findings to staff: prepare a communications package for staff identifying e.g. when TUPE will apply, how transfers will be handled etc.

(g) support the in-house bid: ensure that sufficient professional and qualified resources are provided to assist the in-house team with preparing their bid.

Appendix 6 of this book covers personnel law matters in more detail.

This chapter has attempted to explain the overall process and pointed to some strategic issues. Let's now look at each phase in more detail.

3   Phase 1 – getting started

Chapter 2 sets out the six phases of market testing – this chapter looks in some detail at the first of these, the preliminary phase.

Where are we now?

At the start of this phase, the Department's position is that Ministers have committed themselves to a phased programme (e.g. x per cent of their current command, based on manpower figures, will be market tested in year one, a further x per cent in year two, and so forth). Initial reviews throughout Departments have identified specific areas which, for whatever reason, lend themselves most readily to the first tranche. Some of these areas will have clearly defined boundaries (e.g. the provision of office services at a particular building), while others have more scope for flexibility and will need to be subject to some further thought before a final decision is reached as to what exactly is specified within the particular market testing process (e.g. IT services).

What are we hoping to achieve?

This is certainly a good point, just before the enabling machinery is set up, and the eventual scope and flavour of the actual process is decided, to look at what the process, properly run, might achieve for managers.

Role examination

Market testing calls for a rigorous and critical appraisal of the whole business, and the function, value, quality and cost of each separate element of that business. This approach will not only expose activities which are not now needed at all, or which could more usefully be combined with others. It will also identify which activities are done badly (or well) and which aspects of the business represent particularly good or bad value for money. If a business provides a unique or

Figure 3.1 The six phases of market testing

	PHASE 1 Getting started	PHASE 2 Detailed planning	PHASE 3 Specifications & tender strategy	PHASE 4 The bidding process	PHASE 5 Implementing the results	PHASE 6 Ongoing contract management
Client side activity	Set up management machinery. Make appointments to key groups. Establish outline programmes. Establish policy ground rules. Prepare action plans.	Evaluate proposed activities in more detail. Develop outline tender strategy. Provide training for key staff. Begin market analysis. Select best options for market testing. Get clearance on market test programme and outline tender strategy.	Prepare service specifications and contract documents. Continue to clarify policy ground rules. Identify potential bidders. Identify evaluation criteria. Finalise contract strategy.	Commence formal tendering process. Bidding processes and presentation of bids. Tender evaluation. Post tender negotiations. Detailed evaluation report.	Communicate results. Debrief. Establish future organisation and formalise links. Ensure contract compliance. Introduce contract regime.	Continue contract compliance. Maintain awareness of customer and market. Prepare for next competition.
In-house bid team activity		Identify in-house team. Formulate in-house team strategy.	In-house team review and analysis. Development of in house business plan.	Develop bid strategy. Submit in-house bid.	Mobilise in-house service if successful. Establish client and contractor working systems.	Manage in-house service to budget. Continue to improve performance in readiness for next competition.

→ emerging client/contractor split →

CLIENT/CONTRACTOR SPLIT IN PLACE

particularly good service, how can we capitalise on this and improve, either through competition or otherwise?

Clarification of accountability

One of the essential requirements of market testing is a clear separation of the roles of client and contractor. This is a fairly basic concept, but in the public sector a blurring of managerial lines tends to occur over time. The same manager's post might have acquired, over the years, some responsibilities appropriate to the client, some perhaps more proper to the contractor's side, and yet others where there is no obvious dividing line, or indeed, where the tasks are extraneous to the actual business as such. The market testing process requires a focusing of minds upon managerial accountability, and, having done this, will clear the way for improvements in the accountability structures and in measurable management performance. There is a clear advantage to a business if, in specifying and delineating the line between provision and requirement, creative dynamic tension exists, or can be built into, the process (e.g. an office services manager needs to motivate staff whilst at the same time meeting often demanding performance requirements).

Requirement specification

One of the inherent strengths of the market testing process rests upon the necessity not only to specify what is required (i.e. what the customer requires), but also to set down measurable service levels and performance standards (again, customer driven), for the outputs. It can thus be unequivocally established that the business is then providing a specified type and level of service which is capable of meaningful monitoring, e.g. what the customer actually needs, in the way he wants it, in the quantities he wants it, when he wants it. This is not always the case in many public sector businesses immediately prior to the market testing.

The keen edge of competition

The very process of market testing, properly carried out, brings with it not only the clear management and business advantages outlined above, but the inevitable, and often fierce element of competition. This tends to focus and sharpen minds in such a way as to maximize positive input to the business at all levels. This will, in turn, mean that improved value for money cannot help but to follow.

How can I oil the machinery?

The preceding paragraphs spell out some ways in which the market testing process can, by its very nature, bring out improvements in both performance and value for money. These improvements will, however, be considerably enhanced if a number of important factors are present to establish what might be termed the 'enabling machinery'. A number of these will automatically be built into a soundly based management structure, but it does no harm to set them down at this early stage.

Top-down commitment

This is vital to success. Too often in the past, and with other initiatives in the public sector, this commitment has been lacking, or at best, has been patchy, leaving or encouraging the initiative to fade away or to be allowed to run into the sand. With market testing forming an essential part of the Government's policies, including Prime Ministerial backing and an unequivocal commitment from Ministers, this factor may already be in place. But without a very clear personal commitment from top management there is a real danger that market testing will be seen as an imposed political initiative rather than a proper search for value for money.

Establishment of clear objectives

These should be stretching but achievable. They should not be only organisationally based but personally based as well. They should be set very early in the process by the client side, and monitored closely, with specific procedures for control and pre-set parameters within which to measure achievement.

Departmental guidance

In a number of areas such as financial regimes, personnel and promotion matters, legal constraints, commercial considerations, Trade Union involvements, pay structures etc, there will be doubt and uncertainty. It may be obvious that changes are inevitable, but managers will not necessarily have a clear overview of what these changes might be, how radical they might be, or indeed, what managerial flexibility exists.

I hear the decision has been taken on who will be market tested

They may also be unclear about the process and timing of obtaining Departmental and Treasury approval for flexibilities.

There will thus be a need, on an on-going basis, for specific, accurate and timely guidance from the top in such matters, coupled with specific ground rules. These rules and guidance will provide a structured background against which all parties involved in the market testing process can make decisions, which will then be based upon similar premises. The framework must not only clarify the Department's position upon such matters as changes in financial regimes, different approaches to personnel, pay and performance pay, promotion accommodation and other connected subjects, fresh legal constraints and regulations which might be encountered, and resource allocation. It should also set down Departmental policy where applicable, e.g. broad market testing policy, security considerations, freedom to move to new buildings, buy new equipment or reduce staff.

Supportive resourcing policy

The client side and in-house bidders will need to be sure that the resources exist, and will be made available, to take forward the market testing process in a sensible and structured way. Penny-pinching should not be allowed to interfere with the effectiveness of the process. In different times, market testing is a spend-to-save initiative. The short term pain will be rewarded, and in the case of supporting an in-house bid, is surely a reasonable duty of care for a Department to its loyal employees.

Open policy

It is perhaps inevitable that staff, seeing themselves as under threat, may react particularly negatively if they feel that they are being kept in the dark. Special efforts must be made by the Department and by service managers to ensure that this does not happen. A consistent and structured approach to the regular and continuous dissemination of carefully prepared information is all-important here.

How do we move forward?

Having made the necessary organisational preparations, and ensured that the relevant parts of the machinery are in place and working, how do we take things forward? During this phase, there are several strands of activity involving different groups to be planned for, if not implemented all at once. These include:

- establishment and tasking of an organisation-wide Steering Group;

- establishment and tasking of a market testing unit to provide support and advice to all the market testing teams;

- creation of market testing teams for each project;

- planning for the establishment and tasking of the client side;

- informing and updating TUS and other stakeholders;

- preparation of the project plan to take market testing forward;

- obtaining Ministerial approval.

These are not in chronological order since there are parallel strands, and are certainly not in order of importance.

The Steering Group

Whilst the market testing team carry the responsibility for planning, taking forward and driving through the market testing process, there is a clearly defined need for a higher level oversight of the project. This is perhaps more appropriate to a group which not only looks downwards and is accountable for the market testing team's decisions, but also looks upwards in terms of relaying and clarifying major issues with the top of the office and Ministers.

Amongst the Steering Group's tasks will be:

- determining which specific services should be market tested;

- creating a market testing unit to be a constant source of support and advice;

- accepting and agreeing the terms of reference of the market testing teams and their planning proposals;

- resource and organisational considerations;

31

- monitoring and controlling progress, according to agreed timescales and targets;

- ensuring Ministerial acceptability.

The group will comprise senior members from the Department, its composition will vary from area to area and from project to project. In general terms, it will need to be able to respond sensibly and quickly at various times to problems connected with, for example, finance, personnel, resource allocation, legal matters and procurement. We use the word 'quickly', since it will be vital that the Steering Group decision-taking machinery does not become too cumbersome — there will undoubtedly be occasions in the life of every market testing process when rapid and inequivable decisions are required.

The chair person of the Steering Group will need to be sufficiently senior (objective and independent) to have the capacity to make important decisions without reference, or with the minimum of reference, upwards, yet will need to remain alert and aware in respect of lower level, more detailed considerations.

The market testing unit

The performance of a market testing unit will be a vital factor throughout the whole exercise, since it will be its expertise, experience and energy which will drive the process. Their tasks will include:

- holding the ring between various factions, all of whom will at times feel angry, upset and threatened;

- persuading and cajoling reluctant public servants to go through a series of difficult hoops;

- providing specialist advice; and

- delivering a quality product to an exacting timescale. It will need to combine in appropriate balance the qualities of Solomon, Helen of Troy, Hercules and Attila the Hun.

Where will Departments find such people? The market testing process with all its ramifications, is a fairly new arrival on the public sector scene and as a consequence, there is not a great deal of specific and relevant experience within Departments at present.

The first and arguably most important task is to find a team leader. As a bare minimum, he or she must possess top quality project management skills with proven negotiating ability, and the necessary drive and determination to see things through in the face of considerable, and perhaps high level, opposition.

The team itself will need to encompass a wide variety of skills including good communication and a highly developed analytical ability. Experience in similar areas to that being market tested would be invaluable, as would a background of finance, personnel and procurement.

It is always possible to co-opt others with the necessary experience on to the team at various stages throughout the process, but this brings with it the problems of lack of continuity, commitment to the team, confidentiality and also the danger of conflicts of interest.

In addition, we would see a team member with proven procurement skills as being a particularly useful asset. Aside from being able to provide specialist advice on the whole range of procurement matters which will inevitably arise during a normal market testing process, a procurement background will bring with it added authority and the ability to ensure confidence with EC and GATT directives.

Once established, the team or unit will need to work to precise and specific terms of reference and with clear delegated authorities. These will spell out the accountability, responsibilities and activities throughout the whole process, and will cover such areas as overall planning, strategy development, tendering processes, costings, and eventual implementation.

Market testing teams

Given the size, scope and complexity of most Government Departments, it is unrealistic to expect a single market testing team to oversee and project manage all market tests. The most practical course of action is to appoint a market testing team for each of the market tested activities. This then enables an experienced and knowledgable group of individuals to concentrate effort on individual activities. The work and involvement of an individual market testing team, coupled with advice from the market testing unit should provide the ideal combination for all market tested activities.

The market testing project team is therefore likely to comprise managers from the service activity to be market tested, with specialist input from a market testing unit and other potential sources of advice such as procurement, finance, legal and where appropriate external sources.

In these circumstances, the job of the market testing team could be summarised as follows:

- to organise and mobilise the market test;

- to ensure that the market test takes place within departmental policy guidelines and requirements;

- to ensure that the market test takes place fairly;

- to ensure that client and contractor split separation takes place at the appropriate time;

- to ensure that tender evaluation takes place at the appropriate time to a satisfactory methodology and with the appropriate skill inputs.

More detailed terms of reference for market testing teams are included in Appendix 2.

Conflicts of interest

The market testing process in the public sector is such that at various points, conflicts of interest must inevitably arise. The approach in this book will be simply to highlight the possibility of these when they arise during descriptions of the process. In some cases, conflicts of interest can be minimised by an informed choice of personnel and by the careful allocation of functions, but it is very unlikely in practice to avoid them entirely.

It will happen within the Steering Group. Members of the Group, at a reasonably senior level, will no doubt have their own particular areas of line management responsibility. Since they are members of the Steering Group because of their specific expertise, it is likely that decisions taken in the market testing process will impact directly or indirectly, marginally or considerably, upon members' line functions.

Members will clearly need to strike a balance between the interest and demands of the market testing project, and what will be seen as 'fighting their corner' for their own troops. There must be no ambiguity here. Shades of grey are likely to be tested in the courts.

The client side

Looking ahead to the time when contracts have been let and are in the process of implementation, there will be a clear need for some sort of organisation (which will vary in size according to the type and general requirements of the particular business) to oversee the contract and ensure smooth running and compliance.

This client-side organisation will normally be drawn from within the existing Department and will comprise members of staff with the necessary skills and knowledge to perform the functions envisaged. Even at this early stage, it is most important to anticipate the necessary arrangements to identify, set up, and more importantly, to find the means of resourcing the client-side organisation.

Under the oversight of the Steering Group, the market testing team will have to plan the organisation of the client-side. This will involve establishing the overall organisational structure, setting down its tasks, accountabilities and responsibilities, identifying possible members of the client-side from within the staff, and estimating resource requirements.

**Market Testing
Client-side roles (indicative)**

- Cost the existing service.
- Review current service levels.
- Design contract and specification format and tender strategy.
- Prepare definition of activities and develop outline/draft specification.
- Prepare service specification.
- Design tender process.
- Develop policy on use of equipment and premises.
- Design client management structure.
- Develop tender evaluation model.
- Develop contract award and mobilisation plan.
- Invite tenders.
- Evaluate and award contract.
- Implement contract and contract management arrangements.
- Prepare for next market test.

**Figure 3.2   Indication of best time for client
and in-house bidder split**

Client side roles	In-house roles
• Cost the existing service. • Review current service levels. • Design contract and specification format and tender strategy. • Prepare definition of activities and develop outline/draft specification.	• Agree management. resource and structure. • Check base costings and agree with client. • Highlight policy and specification issues for considerations by client.
• Prepare service specification. • Design tender process. • Develop policy on use of equipment and premises. • Design client management structure. • Develop tender evaluation model. • Develop contract award and mobilisation plan. • Invite tenders. • Evaluate and award contract. • Implement contract and contract management arrangements. • Prepare for next market test.	• Develop preliminary business assessment. • Prepare business development plan. • Prepare provisional submission. • Negotiate changes with staff groups/unions. • Finalise policy position with client managers. • Analyse final specification in detail. • Prepare tender submission. • Prepare mobilisation plan. • Submit tender. • Implement contract if successful.

Should there be an in-house team bid?

The thrust of the 'Competing for Quality' White Paper is for the market testing process to include, under normal circumstances, an in-house team, and for that team to receive every legitimate encouragement from management. Figure 3.2 looks at the best time for a client and in-house bidder split.

However, there are circumstances under which an in-house bid might not be considered appropriate. For instance, the view might be taken that the quality of current service provided is of such a level that it would not be in the public interest to invest the (possibly) substantial amounts required to bring it up to a competitive level. Similarly, the costs of up-dating the technology might be profligate. Or, it might be the case that the actual staff themselves, having seen the alternative possibilities, decide that they would rather 'take their chances' commercially than remain in the Public Sector.

Market Testing
In-house bidder roles (indicative)

- Agree management resource and structure.
- Check base costings and agree with client.
- Highlight policy and specification issues for consideration by client.
- Develop preliminary business assessment.
- Prepare business development plan.
- Prepare provisional submission.
- Negotiate changes with staff groups/unions.
- Finalise policy position with client managers.
- Analyse final specification in detail.
- Prepare tender submission.
- Prepare mobilisation plan.
- Submit tender.
- Implement contract if successful.

Confidentiality and fairness

As the market testing process develops, the in-house team will be bidding against external bidders for what might be, in commercial terms, extremely valuable contracts. The external bidders need to be reassured that the competition is fair and proper (insofar as it can be) right through the process. Any perceived deviation from the norm of fairness will end up being subject to legal action and court appearances. As a consequence, the market testing team, the in-house bid team and the Department itself must from the start, pay attention to this aspect and be aware of the possible consequences at all times. Level playing fields must be created. During the later phases, the establishment of controls over information exchange will be necessary to preserve this essential fairness. But even at this stage, the aspects of confidentiality and fairness and the consequences of any lapses need to be borne very much in mind during the development of necessary links between the in-house team and the market testing team.

TUS and staff consultation

The market testing process will inevitably be seen as a threat by unions and by staff involved in the areas being tested. There will be concern, justified in most instances, about future employment prospects. Staff will be aware of the possibilities of changes to working conditions, pay, personnel policies − in fact the very structures of their working lives. They will be aware that such previously hallowed institutions as pay scales, pay rules, pay structures, postings procedures, promotion procedures, in-built career safe guards, the fast stream, the open structure etc, are all 'up for grabs' and are candidates for change. Even assumptions about the size and shape of the fast stream and the open structure are to some extent threatened by a wide ranging market testing programme.

Fear of the unknown will inevitably make them anxious, and there must be a very real danger that their initial negative feelings towards the process may well spill over into their work and affect the people involved in the market test − to the obvious detriment of the testing process itself.

It therefore makes good sense managerially (and there are additional established obligations in relation to the TUS), to offer what reassurances can be offered in terms of an on-going, structured and comprehensive release of information to both the TUS and to the staff, at various stages in the process. A publicized series of meetings at which staff are allowed to voice concerns without inhibitions; regular consultations where staff representatives feel that they are actively making an input; published progress bulletins; the establishment of an open, available style of conducting business by the market testing team − all these will assist in allaying understandable fears and anxieties. But the realities of a commercially driven and commercially sensitive process constrain the ability to share openly much of the information, until the process provides a final winner and forces consequential decisions. In other words, the game is not over until the music stops. As in musical chairs, it is assumed that not all the players will find a seat.

The project plan

The final step now is the preparation and implementation of a project plan by the market testing team, again supported by advice from the market testing unit. This will cover such matters as potential resource requirements, a broad timetable and internal team responsibilities and activities. This will, in effect, set in motion the actual process itself.

Bearing in mind that whilst the overall programme is known, the final scoping arrangements and packaging are still to be carried out, the plan will in broad terms:

- estimate resource requirements, including the market testing team, the client organisation, internal and external support;

- set down management responsibilities and activities within the market testing team;

- put in place a timetable, with target dates;

- list objectives.

This plan will be submitted to, and be approved by, the Steering Group and will form the basis for action by the market testing team in the future. It may be subject to amendments from time to time, as conditions and circumstances vary. See Figure 3.3.

Figure 3.3   Typical Project Plan

Task	Responsibility	Month 1	2	3	4	...	12
A ORGANISATION							
– Identify key managers (client and in-house team)							
– Nominate authorised officer							
– Determine roles and responsibilities							
– Agree and define scope of service							
B REVIEW CURRENT SERVICE							
– Conduct preliminary assessment							
– Determine key parameters							
– Plan and organise data collection							
– Collect relevant data							
– Produce the service profile							
C COST THE EXISTING SERVICE							
– Identify cost data and source							
– Calculate base cost of current service							
– Provide costing to in-house team							
D ASSESS AND SET SERVICE STANDARDS							
– Identify and agree service objectives							
– Review current service standards							
– Agree and set future performance measures							
E TENDER STRATEGY							
– Develop options for tender strategy							
– Evaluate options							
– Agree tender strategy							
F PREPARE DRAFT SPECIFICATION							
– Identify and agree requirements							
– Write draft specification							
– Consult users and providers							
– Review and revise							

Figure 3.3 Continued

Task	Responsibility	Month 1	2	3	4 ... 12
G SELECT POTENTIAL BIDDERS					
– Prepare information requirements					
– Organise to respond to enquiries					
– Draft and place advertisement					
– Receive and evaluate responses					
– Produce and agree select list					
H PREPARE TENDER DOCUMENTATION					
– Prepare and agree contract conditions					
– Prepare and agree tender conditions					
– Prepare and agree tender schedules					
– Prepare and agree specification					
– Produce invitation to tender documentation					
I INVITE TENDERS					
– Prepare for site visit					
– Invite tenders					
– Site visit by bidders					
J EVALUATE TENDERS					
– Closing date for receipt of bids					
– Evaluate and assess tenders					
– Prepare tender evaluation report					
– Brief tender board					
– Hold tender board interviews					
K AWARD OF CONTRACT					
– Contract negotiations					
– Award contract to external contractor or prepare service level agreement with in-house team					
L MOBILISATION AND MONITORING					
– Prepare written procedures for contractor					
– Provide induction training and familiarisation for external contractors					
– Provide briefing for users on new arrangements					
– Contract start date					
– First review meeting					

41

Ministerial approval

The arrangements for Ministerial approval may vary from one Department to another and are likely to change over time. In the early stages of the market testing initiative Ministers may expect to approve the programme, the detailed market test and the selected contractors.

Over time Ministers may content themselves to approve the overall programme and leave all subsequent decisions to their most senior managers, perhaps requesting progress reports from time to time concerning key achievements.

4 Phase 2 – detailed planning

The last chapter saw the establishment of the various groups necessary to set the market testing process on its way. The market testing team put the wheels in motion by presenting its project plan, which established initial resource requirements, proposed a timetable with target dates, and looked at broadly based objectives.

In this phase, the process gathers momentum prior to the actual specification and tendering phases. In the course of this phase:

- the market testing team will prepare a business analysis;

- the decision will be taken as to the final packaging of the area to be market tested;

- the in-house team will be formed and will begin to develop its strategy.

Information exchange controls

Contained in the current arrangements for market testing within the public service are a number of potential pitfalls in terms of the availability and release of commercially sensitive information. In most basic terms, the market testing team needs to work closely with the current service providers in obtaining and analysing information relevant to the progress of the market testing process. Some of this information will be commercially sensitive while some will have a direct relevance to specific aspects of the competitive tendering process. At the same time however, an in-house team, drawn largely from among those same service providers, is in the process of preparing a competitive bid for the business.

In order to avoid the possible, perhaps accidental, release of commercial information to the in-house team, and the subsequent accusations of unfairness which will undoubtedly follow, a set of formal arrangements and controls needs to be put in place at an early stage. Since it is the market testing team, and the client side who are

Figure 4.1 The six phases of market testing

	PHASE 1 Getting started	PHASE 2 Detailed planning	PHASE 3 Specifications & tender strategy	PHASE 4 The bidding process	PHASE 5 Implementing the results	PHASE 6 Ongoing contract management
Client side activity	Set up management machinery. Make appointments to key groups. Establish outline programmes. Establish policy ground rules. Prepare action plans.	Evaluate proposed activities in more detail. Develop outline tender strategy. Provide training for key staff. Begin market analysis. Select best options for market testing. Get clearance on market test programme and outline tender strategy.	Prepare service specifications and contract documents. Continue to clarify policy ground rules. Identify potential bidders. Identify evaluation criteria. Finalise contract strategy.	Commence formal tendering process. Bidding processes and presentation of bids. Tender evaluation. Post tender negotiations. Detailed evaluation report.	Communicate results. Debrief. Establish future organisation and formalise links. Ensure contract compliance. Introduce contract regime.	Continue contract compliance. Maintain awareness of customer and market. Prepare for next competition.
In-house bid team activity		Identify in-house team. Formulate in-house team strategy.	In-house team review and analysis. Development of in house business plan.	Develop bid strategy. Submit in-house bid.	Mobilise in-house service if successful. Establish client and contractor working systems.	Manage in-house service to budget. Continue to improve performance in readiness for next competition.

CLIENT/CONTRACTOR SPLIT IN PLACE

→ emerging client contractor split →

primarily at risk in this instance, they will need to take the responsibility for the establishment, maintenance and development of these arrangements, and for the setting up of formal, recognised relationships and channels of communication.

All parties must recognise at an early stage that any lapses in, or breaches of, these control arrangements, could have serious consequences and perhaps jeopardise the whole market testing process. External bidders need to be reassured that the process is fair and above board, and the release of advantageous material to the in-house team is an obvious way of demonstrating that this is manifestly not so.

As examples, the market testing team during the current phase will be amassing commercial information about likely external commercial bidders — in effect the competition against the in-house bid. Again, the market testing team will be aware well in advance of the issue of invitations to tender, what decisions have been taken about the market testing process in a number of commercially sensitive areas, eg what specifications will be appropriate, who the likely bidders will be, what the contract strategy is, etc. Such information must not be made available to the in-house team. During any iterative discussions about the specification, the in-house bidder must receive exactly the same treatment, no more and no less, than the others who are involved in the discussions.

In practical terms, from the period of establishment of the market testing and in-house bid teams, up to the final issue of invitations to tender, both sides will have to be aware of the formal information control arrangements which are in force. In addition, both the Steering Group (which may be involved, at different times, with both the market testing team and the in-house team) and any support services which may be involved, should be fully appraised of the relevant arrangements, to avoid any inadvertent release of information.

Once the invitation to tender stage has been reached, then the in-house bid team can, in effect, be treated in exactly the same way as external bidders.

The market testing team

To enable the 'packaging' decision to be soundly, accurately and commercially based, and also, more importantly, to assist in the eventual development of the contract strategy itself, the market testing team will now move on to develop a comprehensive business analysis. This analysis will:

- examine and analyse the current service, including costs and internal dynamics;

- carry out a customer survey to determine present levels of customer satisfaction, and possible future requirements;

- carry out some basic market research to establish the level of demand or interest in the particular business, including the identification of potential bidders;

- in the light of three items above, identify where potential improvements could be made to current processes, including cost implications;

- produce a revised business model with performance indicators/output measures where appropriate, incorporating information drawn from previous activities and including costings;

- form a view as to what options exist for packaging/presentation.

Let's develop each of these a little.

Current service analysis

This analysis would start from the very basic premise of examining the service provided and reaching a view as to whether it is actually necessary, and if so, whether it should be in its present form. Would it make sense, for instance, if it were amalgamated with some other service, or broken down into its constituent parts? As it is at present, what value does it add?

The team would then move on to examine the various processes which actually make up the service, and how they impact upon each other, i.e. the internal dynamics of the business. Linked to this would be a costing exercise, examining the various processes and functions and possibly establishing their relative importance and their relative cost.

These analyses will be useful, not only in increasing the understanding of how the system actually works, and as a consequence, how certain decisions might affect the business as a whole, but also in

enabling the market testing team to form an initial view of the possible packaging and presentation of the area for market testing purposes.

Customer survey

The current service may provide for one customer or for several. The market testing team would carry out a survey utilising a standard questionnaire (where relevant) aimed at establishing levels of customer satisfaction with the currently provided service. Is it what they want? Is it enough, or too much? Is the quality satisfactory? Is it on time?

From this, the team will move on to explore what improvements customers might like to see, whether their future requirements might increase or decrease, their relative priorities in terms of costs/ standards/service delivery.

Market research

This element of the analysis would involve the team in an exercise to make contact with selected commercial providers of similar services, to establish the level of demand and interest in the relevant field.

Face to face meetings probably represent the most fruitful approach and some contractors will certainly be more than willing to discuss how they might go about the business, and offer suggestions as to commercial viability. Whilst the team are likely to draw substantial benefit from exposure to this commercial dimension and valuable lessons can be drawn in terms of market potential, there is a need for caution here.

The market will undoubtedly be aware of the reason behind the research. As a consequence, those approached will, in many cases, be anxious to establish themselves as potential bidders. This is certainly not the object of this exercise, and accordingly meetings should be handled with some caution, i.e. on a without commitment/without prejudice basis and with a formal record being kept of discussions, in case of later difficulties or differences of opinion. Where possible, agreed 'rules of engagement' should be established for dealing with prospective tenderers.

Potential improvements

The team now has extensive background information on the following areas: how the current business actually ticks, how its component parts affect each other, what the relative costings are, what customers think of it, how customers think it could improve, what the future customer demand might be, and what the market potential might be.

This information should enable the team to pin-point areas where improvements might be made to the current service provision, in terms of both costings and of service delivery. These improvements might include not only the areas where, at present, customers have expressed some dissatisfaction, but also those where disproportionate costs might suggest some different organisational arrangements.

As an overlay to this, the team will also be in a position to suggest, in the light of the customer survey, areas where perhaps a different, or differently presented, service might be more appropriate. Estimated costings of these options should also be possible.

Revised business model

Building upon the previous activity, the team is now in a position to produce a revised model of the whole business. This should include not only a number of costed variations of options, but also a structured appraisal of efficiency and maintenance of standards, by means of a system of output measures and performance indicators, where these are appropriate.

Packaging/presentation

This model will be useful in different ways at various stages throughout the remainder of the market testing process. For the moment its usefulness lies in providing the team with the necessary background information (when coupled with what emerged from the market research activities) to put together the most sensible options for recommending which parts of the area should be market tested, which should not, what boundaries should be laid down, and how the package might best be presented — in other words, what is it that we market test, and how do we play it?

The scoping exercise

The preparation of the revised business model and the subsequent suggested packaging have relied to some extent upon information supplied by the present providers. However, the work has been done by the market testing team and the Department's managers have, in the main, not been directly involved in the process so far. Accordingly, it would not be sensible to proceed and to put a final proposal and recommendation to the Steering Group, without some sort of consultative process, since the departmental managers and the TUS will clearly have a view.

At this point, therefore, the team should go through a consultative process, the level and extent of this being determined by the size and complexity of the area involved. Two comments are worth noting:

- firstly, it would normally be at this stage that a degree of 'in-fighting' and political pressures will ensue. A number of managers would clearly see it as advantageous to avoid the market testing process altogether and remain in the comparatively safe haven of the client side. This approach, if successful, seriously limits the opportunity for value for money and for the savings which would otherwise flow from the market testing process.

- secondly, this represents perhaps one of the first occasions on which the information exchange control arrangements mentioned earlier will need to be called into action. Knowledge of the details of potential packaging will obviously be considered a commercial advantage, and as such, the in-house bid team should not be made aware of the options at this stage.

At the end of the consultation process, the market testing team will be in a position – with the dimension of internal management view points having put a final gloss upon the remainder of the detailed knowledge the team has built up – to prepare a report for submission to the Steering Group.

This report, drawing heavily upon the revised business model and the market review, will set out the best options for packaging the area and for presenting it in the most advantageous way to the market so as to ensure the right sort of competition. Where an option includes a potential improvement in, or development of, current services (suggested perhaps by the customer review), the team would set out the relevant costing implications of this course of action. The report would normally favour one option whilst exposing and exploring a number of others.

The Steering Group will normally have the responsibility of signing off the eventual option, or options.

The in-house bid team

As with the setting up of the market testing team, the identification and selection of the in-house bid team leader is of crucial importance to the potential chances of the success of the bid.

Firstly, and most importantly, there is a requirement for considerable and in-depth knowledge/experience of the organisation which is being tested, preferably at more than one level, and certainly at quite a senior level within the organisation. Added to this will be a need for a high degree of management and communication skills, but with evidence of adaptability and flexibility, since the primary need will now be to transpose all these skills into a commercially-based environment. These criteria will, in most cases, narrow the field down considerably and, often, the in-house bid team leader is more or less self-selecting.

What must also be borne in mind here is that whilst the team will be working closely with senior management, and with the consequent need to have their full confidence, it will be vital for the team to be able to look critically (and thus in a way criticise that same senior management) at the current organisation with a view to identifying improvements. This is a delicate path to tread, and one which will call for considerable diplomacy and skill on the part of the team and its leader.

Once the team leader has been identified and is in place, the selection of the rest of the in-house team can proceed. The size of the permanent team will depend upon the size of the areas involved, but the team will need a mix of people with skills in the area and processes being tested, in the procurement/contracts area, the financial area (preferably as a management accountant), and possibly in the personnel/training areas. Other specialist requirements can be drawn upon as and when required (e.g. legal advice).

Ideally, the in-house bid team should consist of managers who will operate the service if the bid is successful. Winning a bid is not just about low pricing. The key management task is to submit a bid which can deliver the quality of service specified at the price submitted. This clearly becomes more difficult as the price gets lower. It is vital that those responsible for the future delivery of the service have ownership of the bid as this will dictate the future availability of resources.

Once established, the in-house team can begin its preparations in earnest. Its principal (and most frantic) endeavours tend to take place later in the process, but in broad terms its aims and objectives are:

- reviewing and analysing current operations and processes with a view to identifying (and quantifying) areas where improvements can be made;

- identifying and assessing potential commercial competitors;

- by means of financial and other models, taking into account possible pay/structure and financial changes and developing a commercial model of the business, upon which the eventual bid can be based;

- preparing and submitting, in accordance with developed strategy, an in-house bid.

During this phase the first two of these aims should be being developed, and Chapter 5 follows on with the preparation of the commercial business model.

Review of current operations

This review has two primary objectives — first, to provide the in-house team with a comprehensive and in-depth analysis of how the current operation works, its strengths and weaknesses, its cost structures, and its internal dynamics. Secondly, by using the analysis and other means, to produce a plan as to how the business might be improved.

The initial phase of this particular process will be an in-depth examination of current procedures, working methods, inter-relationships between different parts of the business, dynamic tensions, cost structures, financial constraints, organisational arrangements, managerial and staff accountabilities and responsibilities. It may well be that background documentation exists which would assist the team in these tasks, or it may be necessary to start from scratch.

Either way, the team will need to prepare fully detailed models of the present workings of the business, in organisational, functional, and financial terms.

These models will then need to be subject to several separate analyses in an effort to identify possible weaknesses and strengths inherent in the structures. Some things may be immediately obvious (e.g. two functions, currently separate, could be combined to improve costings), some less obvious and needing to be carefully teased out by analysis and discussion.

Here the in-house team has the benefit of being part of the current provider structure, and as such, will have access to the background and expertise which will have been built up, probably over a number of years. This can, however, be a two edged sword if care in approach is not exercised — long-term familiarity with a system does not necessarily go hand-in-hand with flexibility of thought.

There would be considerable merit at this point, and again the fact that the team are part of the providers would tend to oil the wheels, in approaching the customer(s). Such an approach would have similar purposes to that which would be made to the customer by the market testing team — i.e. to gauge the present level of customer satisfaction with all aspects of the service provided (appropriateness, quality, quantity, timeliness etc.) and then to seek customers' views upon possible improvements and foreseeable future requirements.

Commercial confidentiality, however, and the paramount need to maintain fairness and propriety, would mean that the in-house team approach would normally need to be totally separate from the market testing team's exercise.

As a next stage, the team must move on to build a series of models incorporating possible improvements to the present operation, based partly on the previous analyses — the strengths/weaknesses in particular, and partly upon perceived future requirements. Incorporated in these models would be any changes (flowing from the market testing process) to Departmental arrangements of which the team are aware, e.g. any additional freedom envisaged within the financial provisions, changes in policy constraints or security.

The models would explore the various options for improvements at various levels and within different functions, and an important feature of the modelling process will be detailed cost structures. In this way, the team can build up a number of scenarios supported by modelled evidence, indicating where efforts might best be directed to produce better value for money by means of improved efficiency or service delivery, either in reduced costs, or in producing more for the same costs (or less) or indeed in producing proportionally more for higher costs.

The proposals which flow from the modelling processes will thus be soundly based, but will need also to be practical and realistic, and could cover a range of possible improvements. Flexibility in approach is the key at this stage, particularly since the terms and requirements of the eventual invitation to tender may preclude some of the possible improvements which the team will have identified.

Identifying and assessing potential commercial competitors

Although the in-house team will not at this stage be aware of who the likely competitors will be, or indeed how many there might be, there remains a clear need to develop a market and competitor awareness since, in the final issue, the success or failure of the in-house team bid will be judged in commercial terms against commercially based competition.

How do the team go about this? Well, aside from the background information which will be readily available as pointers to the particular market involved (e.g. trade journals, targeted magazines, specific newspaper coverages, and the like), there is the Department's own procurement staff. They will have not only personal background information upon the market place, but will, possibly more valuably, have a network of personal commercial contacts who should be able to provide clearly-focused information within the particular market areas.

Additionally, other parts of the Department, or indeed other Departments, may well have historical knowledge of potential competitors and their capabilities from previous experiences, or previous open tender processes.

From these various sources and any others which might apply to the particular area in which the business is located, a picture can be assembled of the potential market place in which the in-house team would be fighting for a position.

There should be two aspects to this. First, a developed view of the number and range of potential competitors with, where possible, an assessment of such features as:

- their track record;

- their other activities;

- their size and structure;

- their particular niche in the market place;

- their pricing strategies;

- any known strengths and weaknesses;

- their financial state and current viability.

As the second part of this exercise, and based upon what emerges from the first part, the team will then need to take a view as to where they would stand commercially, were they to seek to take a place in the market. This will call for a broad comparison across the perceived market, between the businesses current service standards, range of products, price ranges, strengths, weaknesses etc, and similarly-based assessments of likely competitors' products.

Besides giving the team a feel for the market and where their business might fit into the overall picture, this process has the added advantage that it will serve to delineate where clear advantages exist, in either direction, and will give the team an early indication of where they might need to focus some of their efforts to overcome any such disadvantages, or indeed, to strengthen and underline any advantages they themselves may have.

By the end of this phase, the in-house team will have developed models analysing the current business and identifying a raft of possible improvements, complete with cost/saving implications. In addition, they will have formed a fairly detailed view of the potential market place, where they might aim to place themselves in that market place, and what they might have to focus upon to improve their chances. Perhaps more importantly, by the very process of looking at things commercial, and in a commercial way, the team will have begun the process which it will need to develop and improve upon considerably later — i.e. thinking commercially rather than internally.

Influencing the process

Quite apart from increasing their information base and adapting their thinking along commercial lines, the in-house team has an opportunity to influence the market testing process, to attempt, legitimately, to steer the market testing team's thoughts along lines possibly more advantageous to themselves, by means of day-to-day discussions, and by the submission of papers and other documents. Many of the key players in deciding packaging, specifications, evaluation criteria and other vital elements of the market testing process will be known to the in-house team and will, in fact, be involved with them on a day-to-day basis in the run-up to the letting of contracts. There is no reason why the in-house team cannot, without any fear of allegations of unfairness, make legitimate and helpful suggestions as to how they might see the thrust of, say, the specification going, or advantages which they might see in certain packaging arrangements. After all, the commercial firms who may eventually provide the competition, may be attempting to do exactly the same thing using their own methods.

This use of influence is an important weapon in the rather limited armoury of the in-house team.

External assistance

What we have described above as necessary tasks for the in-house team call for a fairly high degree of specialised skills in terms of analytical processing, model development, etc. Is it fair, then, to ask the team to perform critical tasks, the outcome of which might decide their futures, when they may not have had specific training, or possibly do not have the necessary specialist skills within the team?

There is, no doubt, an awareness amongst Departments and certainly amongst external bidders, of the high level of added value in getting the right skills to help at specific stages in the market testing process.

The decisions as to what, if any, support, should be provided to in-house bidders rest with the Departmental managers. If an in-house team makes a request, the choices range from refusal, through providing Departmental specialist support (e.g. O&M staff), to the use of experienced consultants.

Most senior managers now believe that there is a 'duty of care' element here which, it can be argued, Departments owe to their staff in order to give them as good a fighting chance in open competition as possible.

TUS and staff communications

A continuing feature of this phase will be the dissemination of information to, and consultation with, the TUS and with interested staff, along similar lines to those which we outlined in Chapter 3. The involvement at this stage of contacts with customers and with commercial activities will need particularly careful explanation to set minds at rest as to motives, hidden agendas etc.

Commercial firms

By this time managers can expect the potential front-runners in any anticipated competition to be making a strong play for recognition. They might well be approaching the identified key players in the Department and in the market testing team by putting forward their own views, and offering to help in any way they can, whilst at the same time attempting to ensure that the market testing process was directed along the path most advantageous to themselves. They would by now, have decided:

- what is the opportunity;

- what they wanted from it;

- how they could get what they wanted;

- how best to influence matters in their direction.

Their marketing pitch would be well developed and their help and suggestions might encompass, not only the provision of useful information and commercial guidance, but also suggestions on packaging, specification, evaluation criteria and the like. They would be attempting to appear credible and realistic, aware of course, that their competitors would probably be going through the same motions. How successful they might have been will be reflected in the actual packaging and specification of the business.

5 Phase 3 — specifications and tender strategy

We have now reached the stage where we know what we are market testing. Our next phase is to transform this knowledge and package the requirements in such a way that both the client and any potential bidders are fully aware of what is being asked for.

Specification phase

Several important but distinct activities take place during this phase, activities perhaps best carried out primarily by the market testing team, but with some early inputs to the process from the prospective in-house bidders.

Lets take a look at the market testing team inputs at this time. These are:

- clarification of policy ground rules;

- writing of specifications;

- identifying potential bidders;

- finalising contract strategy and tender documentation.

Clarification of policy ground rules

Phase 1 covered the aspects of establishing basic policy ground rules. These should normally exist within civil service Departments and will cover such areas as general market testing policy, information availability, security, recruitment, postings and personnel policies, and any particularly sensitive subjects, perhaps specific to the Department involved. They will, in broad terms, serve to:

Figure 5.1   The six phases of market testing

	PHASE 1 Getting started	PHASE 2 Detailed planning	PHASE 3 Specifications & tender strategy	PHASE 4 The bidding process	PHASE 5 Implementing the results	PHASE 6 Ongoing contract management
Client side activity	Set up management machinery. Make appointments to key groups. Establish outline programmes. Establish policy ground rules. Prepare action plans.	Evaluate proposed activities in more detail. Develop outline tender strategy. Provide training for key staff. Begin market analysis. Select best options for market testing. Get clearance on market test programme and outline tender strategy.	Prepare service specifications and contract document. Continue to clarify policy ground rules. Identify potential bidders. Identify evaluation criteria. Finalise contract strategy.	Commence formal tendering process. Bidding processes and presentation of bids. Tender evaluation. Post tender negotiations. Detailed evaluation report.	Communicate results. Debrief. Establish future organisation and formalise links. Ensure contract compliance. Introduce contract regime.	Continue contract compliance. Maintain awareness of customer and market. Prepare for next competition.
In-house bid team activity		Identify in-house team. Formulate in-house team strategy.	In-house team review and analysis. Development of in house business plan.	Develop bid strategy. Submit in-house bid.	Mobilise in-house service if successful. Establish client and contractor working systems.	Manage in-house service to budget. Continue to improve performance in readiness for next competition.

→ emerging client/contractor split →

CLIENT/CONTRACTOR SPLIT IN PLACE

- alert market testing teams to important and specific issues which need to be borne in mind;

- ensure that the approach to staff and TUS is consistent;

- ensure a structured approach to common issues throughout the Department.

As a precautionary measure at this important stage, the market testing team will simply need to update itself on the particular issues and how they might impact upon the preparation of tender specifications and contract strategy, to ensure that any relevant aspects of Departmental policy are reflected in their approach.

Writing specifications

The specification document

The specification is one of the key documents of the market testing process. It forms part of the contract documents which will also include:

- invitation to tender;

- conditions of contract;

- tender schedules.

A good specification will set out requirements in terms of functions and performance standards rather than resources and methods.

Purpose of the specification

The specification is the most detailed of the contract documents. It is the description of the service required to meet a particular need. Its purpose is to define the requirements to which the service has to conform and against which the service will be monitored.

The specification is the core document in the tendering process and care and skill should be used in preparing it. It must describe precisely and unambiguously the work or service required, outputs to be produced, and standards to be achieved.

Clear and precise specifications encourage keen prices and make contracts easier to manage. A poorly written document with weak definitions will result in an unsatisfactory service and higher costs. A poor specification can never be remedied by a tightly drawn contract.

Producing the specification

The production of a specification is a major task, particularly when a large amount of data about the service has to be collected. In many cases this will be for the first time. In addition, where the activities to be market tested are large or complex, wide-ranging consultation and agreement may be needed with a number of users.

Producing a good specification involves five essential steps:

- analysing service needs;

- collating all related data on quantities and timing;

- designing a structure for the document;

- writing the specification;

- review and approval.

Each step is described below.

Analysing service needs

Before writing the specification it is necessary to have completed other essential parts of the market testing process:

- the preparation of an up-to-date profile of the service. This will provide details of how the activities are currently being performed, the quantity of work being produced and the quality of service being provided;

- the setting of future service standards in consultation with customers of the service. Performance standards should be measurable to make monitoring easier, and associated with outcomes or results rather than the inputs or resources employed;

- consideration of the possible tender strategy and contract options;

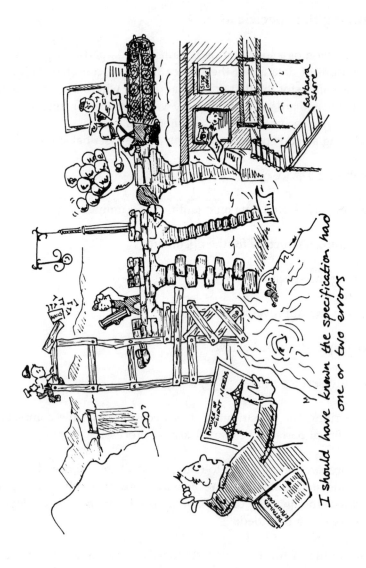

- examination of service levels which define the breadth of service required;

- determination of future work volumes, which may not be the same as in the past. It is important to consult customers of the service about future trends in the quantity of work that will be required. If there are uncertainties, then a clear indication of the likely workload variations should be determined and a pricing structure adopted which will cater for these.

Collating all related data on quantities and timing

The specification must tell potential contractors clearly what they are required to provide. A good specification will not be unduly prescriptive about the resources to be employed or the methods to be used but will define the job required in terms of:

- the functions to be performed (scope of service);

- the outputs sought (quantities);

- the performance required (quality).

The specification should not prescribe current processes, practices and methods of working as this will prevent innovation in service delivery by the contractor.

Whilst it will often be helpful to present historic data about work volumes and service patterns from the service profile, the purpose of the specification is to define future requirements.

A good specification will usually also include:

- a brief background to the service including its history, where it fits into the organisation, or how the requirement has arisen;

- details of the accommodation, equipment and materials that will be supplied or offered, if any;

- criteria against which contractor's performance will be monitored and the means of monitoring;

- contractor's responsibilities at the conclusion of the contract to ensure a smooth handover to a new contractor;

- the responsibilities of the users to whom the contractor will provide the service.

The specification should contain sufficient information to enable potential contractors to determine and make accurate costings of the service. Contractors should have no doubt about the objectives for the service and what is expected of them.

Designing a structure for the document

A variety of formats may be used for the structure of specification documents. There are no fixed rules. Because each specification reflects a different requirement, the structure must fit the need. The actual structure and headings will therefore vary with the type of service being market tested.

The key to it all is to be logical. Address the most important features of the service first, ensure that the contents of sections do not overlap and define the requirement fully so that no essential information is left out.

As a first step it is a good idea to prepare an outline structure setting out the main headings, listing the contents under each main heading and put detailed information and data into appendices. The overriding concern is for the requirements to be fully and clearly defined and not open to misinterpretation.

The exact structure of the specification will depend on the type, nature and complexity of the services to be provided. Each specification is therefore different and must always be individually written.

Writing the specification

It is difficult to write a specification in one step. It is best to produce it in several stages, with consultation and agreement at each point:

- agree the structure for the document. Prepare an outline structure and agree it with users of the service;

- write a first draft. Use the structure as a guide and leave gaps for detail to be filled in. Be prepared to use the structure flexibly — you may find that in writing the draft you want to re-order the content;

- circulate the draft among the users of the service for their comments;

- write a second draft. Following consultation on the first draft prepare a second version incorporating agreed amendments and additions. This can then form the basis of the final version.

HALLMARKS OF GOOD SPECIFICATIONS

- Document logically structured with no overlap of sections.
- Simple language and no jargon.
- Terms, abbreviations and acronyms defined.
- Words and expressions understandable.
- Concise but clear meanings.
- Non-repetitive.
- Attractive format to encourage reading by contractors.
- Each section and paragraph numbered using a logical and consistent numbering method.
- Good use of tables, appendices and diagrams if these help to explain the requirement more clearly.

High level versus low level specifications

High level specifications can be appropriate where there exists a high degree of uncertainty or risk, where you are looking for novel and contentious solutions without constraining the contractors methodology or broad approach. High level specifications can produce better value for money solutions, since contractors can deliver flexibly and innovatively to minimise costs.

Low level specifications are appropriate where the requirement is measurable and has become the basis for output measures or performance indicators.

Existing specifications for similar services are often a useful guide on what to include but should never be copied without considering the services and standards required.

Review and approval

It is beneficial to have the final version read by someone who is unfamiliar with the exercise but who understands the requirements. This often highlights shortcomings such as ambiguity, imprecession and gaps in requirements.

Before specifications are issued as part of tender documentation, they must be formally approved by an individual with delegated responsibility, who should, if necessary consult user representatives. The approval process will vary in different organisations but could include the following:

- that the requirement is effectively defined in the specification;

- that the specification is free from bias;

- that client managers accept responsibility for the use of the specification.

PREPARING A SPECIFICATION – CHECKLIST

- Prepare a plan for producing the specification.
- Produce and agree an outline structure for the document.
- Identify the information that will be required to be collected.
- Prepare a profile of the service.
- Review and set performance standards with users of the service.
- Define the service in terms of the results and performance required – try to avoid prescribing inputs, resources and processes.
- Write the specification in plain language and try to avoid technical or official expressions.
- Consult users of the service at each step to ensure that the specification meets their requirements.
- Get the specification approved in good time for incorporation in the contract documentation.

Legal constraints

A word of warning here on one of the legal constraints relative to specifications. The existence of public procurement law means that if the specification is drawn up in such a way that only one provider can in fact provide, then that in itself is unlawful and could be challenged in the courts. This is particularly relevant where the specification is such that only the in-house provider can satisfy the requirements –

in this case others can, and given the amount involved, will, call foul. Appendix 5 gives an overview of public procurement law in market testing and a summary chart is shown in Figure 5.2.

Non-compliant tenders

At this point it is worth touching upon the subject on non-compliant tenders, that is, tenders which deliberately do not fulfil the specification but which bidders themselves envisage as providing what is required in a different, possibly cheaper, way. Each case will clearly vary. The first question to be answered is, if this approach provides what I want, why did my specification not allow for it? And then, how do I know the non compliant tender will actually provide what I want?

This is a fraught but interesting area and one which needs very careful evaluation before proceeding. Having said that, it may well be, on occasion, a means to providing better value for money, which is after all one of the main thrusts of market testing.

Select tender lists

The use of select tender lists, and/or pre-qualification of potential contractors is advisable in most market tests. Such processes are accepted by industry and have benefits to both sides, on the one hand, in terms of an assessment being made available revealing the contractors readiness and capability to deliver, and on the other, enabling the contractors to be aware of requirements and consequently focus their efforts most usefully. One issue which needs to be considered carefully is the number of organisations who should be invited to tender. If you invite too many then you could end up with a long and tortuous evaluation. If it becomes known that a large number of competitors have been invited, then some will lose interest if they see their chances of winning as small. Whilst there is no ideal number of tenders to invite because markets change, a general guideline to work to is between 7–10 tenderers.

Advertising for interest

Advertising the intention to market test an activity is the most suitable method to assist with the identification of potential tenderers. The alternative is to conduct a thorough search of company

Figure 5.2 Overview of Public Procurement Law

	SUPPLIES	WORKS	UTILITIES	SERVICES
SOURCES OF LAW	• EC Supplies Directive (77/62/EEC as amended by 88/295/EEC) • GATT Government Procurement Agreement • UK Public Supply Contracts Regulations 1991 (SI 1991 No 2679) • Consolidation of EC Supplies Directive (93/36/EEC)	• EC Works Directive (71/305/EEC as amended by 89/440/EEC) • UK Public Works Contracts Regulations 1991 (SE 1991 No 2680) • Consolidation of EC Works Directive (93/37/EEC)	• EC Utilities (formerly Excluded Sectors) Directive (90/531/EEC) • Utilities Supply and Works Contracts Regulations 1992 (SE 1992 No 3279)	• EC Services Directive (92/50/EEC) • EC Services (Utilities) Directive (93/38/EEC)
CONTRACTING AUTHORITIES	• For EC purposes: central, regional and local government and certain other quasi-governmental bodies • For GATT purposes: central government, including NHS authorities • Excluded sectors: energy, water, transport and telecommunications (now subject to the Utilities Supply and Works Contracts Regulations 1992)	Central, regional and local government, including NHS authorities and certain other quasi-governmental bodies (excluding bodies in the energy, water and transport sectors and telecommunications sector)	Public bodies and other entities in the energy, water, transport and telecommunications sectors	• Central, regional and local government, and certain other quasi-governmental bodies • Public bodies and other entities in the energy, water, transport and telecommunications sectors
TYPES OF CONTRACT	Public supply contracts, including hardware and software but not services	Contracts for building and civil engineering projects	Utilities supply contracts and utilities works contracts	Contracts not covered by EC Supplies Directive or EC Works Directive
THRESHOLD	• For regional and local government: 200,000 ECUs (£141,431) • For central government, including NHS authorities: 125,576 ECUs/ 130,000 SDRs (£88,802)	5 million ECUs (£3,535,775)	• Utilities supply contracts in telecommunications sector: 600,000 ECUs (£424,293) • Utilities supply contracts in other regulated sectors: 400,000 ECUs (£282,862) • Utilities works contracts: 5 million ECUs (£3,535,775)	For bodies covered by the EC Services Directive: – 200,000 ECUs (£141,431) For bodies covered by the EC Utilities Directive: – 600,000 ECUs (£424,293) in the telecommunications sector – 400,000 ECUs (£282,862) in other excluded sectors
IMPLEMENTATION DATES	Already implemented	Already implemented	1 January 1993 except in Spain (1 January 1996), Greece and Portugal (1 January 1998)	• EC Services Directive: 1 July 1993 • EC Services (Utilities) Directive: mid-1994 except in Spain (1 January 1996), Greece and Portugal (1 January 1998)

databases and surveys to draw up a list of firms that might tender for the contract. This is time-consuming and costly, and key players may be overlooked who later express legitimate concern that they were omitted.

Where to advertise

Advertising is an open process and is the most effective way to make the maximum number of potential tenderers aware of a contract. The intention to invite tenders for the provision of services may be advertised in a range of publications including local newspapers which have a wide readership, relevant trade publications and national newspapers depending on the size and nature of the service.

In addition there may also be a requirement to place a notice in the Official Journal of the European Community (OJEC).

Experience has shown that the use of both newspapers and trade publications achieves a good response. Many daily newspapers, for example, publish advertisements relating to particular business sectors or services on certain days of the week. They may also have various classified or business-to-business sections where it may be most appropriate to place the advertisement.

The advertisement

The advertisement should state the salient points of the proposed contract and invite contractors to register their interest by a specific closing date. The advertisement should indicate as a minimum:

- a brief description of the type of work;

- the scope and size of the proposed contract;

- the anticipated tender invitation date and contract start date;

- a request for contractors to respond by a specified closing date;

- the address to which contractors should respond.

ADVERTISING FOR INTEREST – CHECKLIST

- Consider whether advertising is likely to be the most effective way of identifying a large field of potential candidates.
- Select the publications in which to advertise including OJEC where applicable.
- Contact the publications.
- Prepare and agree the advertisement.
- Nominate an individual to handle responses to the advertising.
- Place the advertisement.
- Record responses and issue questionnaire to interested parties.

Selecting potential bidders

The list of contractors to be selected to submit tenders should be chosen from those who express interest in response to the advertisement.

Advertising is likely to generate interest from a large number of contractors. Keen competition for the services to be market tested is good, but it is undesirable to invite tenders from every firm that expresses interest, because proper evaluation of a large number of bids is demanding and costly for contractors who prepare unsuccessful bids.

Generally the aim should be to choose no more than 7–10 (including the in-house contractor) to submit bids. The selection should be based on the evaluation of information about a contractor's capability to perform and complete the contract. This will be indicated by information provided by interested contractors about their company, their technical capability and financial stability. The best way of getting these details is to ask potential bidders to complete a pre-tender questionnaire or submit information requested in the advertisement.

Selection process

A large number of contractors may express interest, and it will be necessary to evaluate the responses in detail to reduce the number invited to tender to a manageable level. This is known as the select list.

An evaluation team should be formed to undertake the selection process. A wide range of expertise will be required by the team, including technical expertise the service being tested and the assessment of the trading and financial stability of companies. The team should recommend which contractors are placed on the select list to be invited to bid.

Selection criteria

The criteria for evaluating potential tenderers should be a combination of technical capability and financial status. Pricing issues are irrelevant at this stage. Once the specified closing date has passed, the following steps offer useful guidelines:

- check and record the number of responses received;

- undertake an initial assessment of each questionnaire received to check compliance;

- reject applications which are clearly unacceptable on the basis of the initial assessment;

- undertake a comprehensive assessment of each remaining application as follows:

- technical capability;

- financial status.

- assess which contractors are the most suitable by grading according to the preferred criteria.

Financial checks

Substantial effort is required to assess the financial viability of contractors. The checks should be made on the basis of a full financial assessment of each company using external information databases where appropriate. In addition to the financial checks, reference enquiries for at least two contracts operated by each applicant may also be appropriate to obtain.

As you are aware, we are now tendering for long-term prisoners

Reporting and approval process

The evaluation team should prepare a report based on the assessment of technical capability and financial stability. This should form the recommended select list of contractors.

Unsuccessful applicants

Letters should be sent to all unsuccessful applicants informing them of the decision. Care and discretion should be exercised in discussing specific reasons for rejection of an application with contractors.

Care should be taken to ensure total compliance with EC/GATT regulations.

PRE-TENDER SELECTION CHECKLIST

- Review the pre-selection questionnaire.
- Send the questionnaire to contractors who express an interest.
- Keep a record of questionnaires issued and returned.
- Summarise the list of completed questionnaires.
- Establish and brief a pre-selection evaluation team.
- Perform an initial check on questionnaires and reject those providing insufficient information.
- Undertake a technical assessment of the capability of each potential contractor.
- Assess the financial status of each potential contractor.
- Request financial checks and take references for the short list of potential contractors.
- Prepare a select list report.

Finalisation of tender strategy

The key issues here are size of package, how many packages and length of contract. Many public sector services are provided on a national basis through a network of geographical locations. When market testing occurs there are choices on whether to go for a national package and contract, or a series of regional or linked contracts. If a series of regional or linked contract packages are offered, then contractors may be given an opportunity to bid for individual or multiple contracts.

Choice of strategy in this respect will influence the type and strength of contractor. A national contract will attract large organisations whereas regionally-based contracts will possibly attract large national companies and smaller regionally-based organisations.

Contract length is a further aspect which is worth consideration on its own merits. Possible contract length will vary from a minimum of twelve months, through three years, five years, seven years and even up to ten year periods and beyond. What are the advantages and disadvantages?

To some extent, the contract length will be influenced by the business itself − where basic routine tasks such as cleaning, office keeping or security guarding are involved, when a short-term, highly specific contract will be appropriate.

In other types of business, where perhaps the opportunities for flexibility and innovation are greater, then longer-term contracts will serve the purpose better.

TENDER STRATEGY CHECKLIST

- Identify the factors which will define the size of the contract (volume of work, geographical coverage, organisational boundaries).
- Assess the advantages and disadvantages of having one or more contracts.
- Decide and agree the size and number of contracts.
- Determine the type of contract that will best meet the service objectives.
- Decide what accommodation or equipment will be offered to contractors.
- Determine responsibilities for key aspects such as maintenance, cleaning and repair of accommodation and equipment.
- Consider how long the contract period should be.
- Assess the range of functions to be put together into a single contract package.
- Assess the options for pricing the work required.
- Formulate and agree the tender strategy: size, scope, duration, packaging and pricing method.

From an outside contractors viewpoint, he will be making a

considerable investment, in resource terms, in the business. The longer the period of contract, the longer he has to recover these start up and investment costs, and the greater the opportunity of value for money within the terms of the contract. So, in broad terms, a longer contract length will be of advantage to the outside contractor and will allow him to develop his investment policies more cost effectively, whilst a shorter contract length will be advantageous to the in-house bidder, who will have a much lower investment profile.

Contract conditions

Contract conditions ideally provide the practical link between the specification and the physical translation of requirements. The contract conditions form the legal basis of the agreement between the client and contractor and will cover such aspects as:

- payment arrangements;

- pricing arrangements;

- allocated responsibilities for provision of services;

- responsibilities for data management;

- control procedures;

- security considerations;

- statutory responsibilities.

Formal approval

Phase 1 of the market testing process saw the setting up of the Steering Group, one of whose functions was the setting and over-seeing of contract strategy. It is now the time for such formal finalisation, before moving on to the operation of the tender documents.

There would normally be two thrusts to what is presented for endorsement at this stage. First, in terms of the contract itself, the strategy will encompass:

- the type of contract to be utilised;

- the list of bidders, final selection of which is explained in the previous paragraphs;

- a proposed timescale for the tendering process itself;

- formal approval of the constitution and terms of reference of the Evaluation Panel, together with its specified (and published) evaluation criteria.

The second element can be less practical and more conceptual, and will be, in effect, a forward look at how the client organisation might take shape once the contracts are let. It is important at this stage to get formal Steering Group approval, since the subject of resource allocation and commitment of funds will necessarily form part of the concept. Since the timescale involved can possibly be as long as, or slightly longer than, the timescale envisaged for the tendering process, there will be a need to make a start at this point in time, in order to avoid unnecessary delays later.

The sort of things to consider putting before the Steering Group would include:

- the shape and size of the client organisation needed to take forward the contract oversight, once the tendering processes have reached their conclusion;

- how the present organisation might be transformed, and on what phase timescale, into what is required in the future (this will include the subjects of training, relocation etc);

- what financial and management information systems might need to be set up to oversee contract compliance.

In the final event, the Steering Group must be content that the contract arrangements are the best available in the circumstances, and that the necessary formal planning to take forward the eventual contract is comprehensive and sound.

TUS staff update

As mentioned in the previous chapters, it is most important to keep the TUS and interested staff fully informed on the progress of the market testing process. It is particularly so during this phase, since staff will be aware of the contact and the industry meetings taking place which will occur in the course of the dialogues, and any natural suspicions need to be allayed immediately.

In-house bidders

Where does the team stand now?

At this stage, the requirement is to pull together all the teams previous analyses and activities, and prepare the all-embracing business model which will help to form the basis for the bid. This is the team's last chance prior to the actual bidding/tendering process to get their act in order. What the team should have done so far is to allocate responsibilities and fix upon an organisational and management shape for the future. It should have learned how to adapt its thinking towards business and the market place, rather than traditional internally-based approaches. It will have formed an awareness of the likely competition and its possible strategies. It will have completed an initial business and financial analysis, and have identified opportunities for improvement upon the present performance. It will be clear what freedoms it has, if any, to introduce flexibility and innovation to its proposals.

What is required?

In broad terms the team must, on the basis of its analysis of the current business (including costings, work levels, work flows, history, predictions, organisational structures, etc) take a leap forward and translate all this on to a commercial basis which is both a viable and competitive. Clearly the approach will need to be based differently according to the size and commercial nature of the undertaking. In some instances, the amount of 'commercial-think' required will be greater than others. Elsewhere it may be that traditional, tried and tested methods will prove to be the most effective. Either way, the team's thinking will need to become more commercial. In practical terms, the team must construct a model of what they think the future organisation will look like on a commercial basis.

The purpose of the model would be to set out in an understandable way the perceived commercial dynamics of the structure, and to provide vital insights into the possible costs and resource implications of future decisions. Not an easy task, and one which would call for specific expertise which, if the team did not already possess it, would need to be brought in from outside.

Preparing the business plan

To achieve a viable in-house unit it is essential that the in-house team prepares and implements a realistic and achievable business plan. This will be a complex process but successful completion of this task will provide a firm foundation for preparing and operating a successful in-house business unit.

The process of preparing business plans is well known in the private sector and the principles can be readily adapted to the needs to the public sector. The business planning process can have significant benefits in terms of identifying at an early stage in the process, the major issues and problem areas that will need to be addressed by managers and staff in preparing their bids.

Business planning is essentially the process of asking and answering a series of key questions about the way in which the business will be operated in the future. The key advantages of the business planning process are that it:

- improves accountability;

- establishes a common sense of purpose;

- produces a tangible plan of action with clear deliverables, timescales and costings;

- forces the focus on what can be achieved;

- enables planning and development of the business and its staff.

Structure, timetable and responsibilities

The preparation of a successful business plan will revolve around three key aspects: the structure of the plan, the timescale over which it will be initially be prepared and the allocation of responsibilities for the preparation of the plan. These are discussed in greater detail in the following paragraphs.

Structure

The structure of the business plan will contain four key sections. These are discussed in greater detail below but will essentially comprise of:

- introduction and background;

- business review;

- strategic aims and objectives;

- action and implementation plan.

Whilst the structure of the business plan should remain generally fixed, the plan itself will change over time. A key factor in successful business planning is the continuous review and updating of information to enable the plan to reflect current circumstances. It is pointless implementing actions if the basis on which the decisions have been made is no longer valid. Consequently, continuous review and assessment is a key factor in the business planning process.

Timetable

We have already noted that the business plan should be seen as a continuously updated document. However, it is important to set a rigid timescale for its initial production. It is generally considered that a period of no more than six weeks should be allowed from commencing the exercise to the production of the first draft of the business plan. Whilst this may need to be reviewed and updated, it should be a comprehensive document which includes all the key elements.

Responsibilities

Overall responsibility for the preparation of the business plan should be allocated to one person. This person should then delegate specific tasks to members of the in-house team as appropriate, attempting where possible to ensure that discrete areas of work are allocated. It is important that the members of the team chosen to undertake preparation of specific elements of the business plan should clearly understand their task and have a good understanding of the relevant topic.

Developing the business plan

The overall structure of the business plan was outlined above. This section of the manual details the key elements that will need to be considered.

Introduction and background

The purpose of this section is to provide a short and focused review of the current business environment as it is likely to affect the operation. It sets a context for the detailed business plan by providing some key steps and major factors.

This section of the business plan would seek to cover the following:

- overall purpose of the service;

- outline service descriptions and budgets;

- economic situation and forecast;

- market and competitor analysis;

- legislative and internal constraints.

It should be stressed that this part of the business plan is only an overview and the substantial detail will be contained in the main plan.

Business review

It is necessary to thoroughly review the operation of the in-house service and the external factors which will affect it. Subsequently an assessment can be made of the strategic strengths and weaknesses of the business when compared with potential competitors. This part of the business plan can be divided into three key areas:

- internal assessment;

- external assessment;

- SWOT analysis.

The internal assessment will be a review of the operation and provision of current services. It should include, for example, a full examination of the organisation and management structure comprising staff numbers, supervisory ratios and responsibilities, and should include organisation charts where appropriate. In addition, it should look at the culture within the organisation in terms of the management styles, attitudes and working environment. The third area to be considered should be the staff, involving an examination of skill levels, current productivity and performance and the potential for further development. In this respect human resource and performance measurement records should be used to assess current levels.

The internal operational review should next focus on the range and type of services which are provided, and attempt to define clearly the parameters of the service in much the same way as when the service profile was produced. The cost of the services should also be investigated in depth, including levels of funding and individual activity costing. This will require full analysis of budgets and trading accounts involving detailed analysis of costing methods. The final aspects of the internal review will be an analysis of the current systems used to manage the business, such as charging systems, trading accounts and management control information.

The next stage of the business review is to undertake an assessment of the external factors which will have an influence on the business. This will involve a full competitor analysis. The key elements in the external assessment are:

- market
  - size
  - characteristics
  - demand patterns
  - current market share

- suppliers
  - past performance
  - options for new suppliers

- customers
  - public/customer image and perception
  - customer needs
  - priorities
  - satisfaction criteria

- legislation/constraints
  - recent changes and implications
  - anticipated or probable changes

- funding   – internal markets
  - external sources
  - other alternatives

One of the most important elements of the external review is the competitor assessment. This should involve a full review of the likely competition on a local, regional and national basis and should also attempt to identify new or potential entrants to the business area. For each competitor a data-base should be constructed of key information, specifically:

- operating methods;

- current contracts;

- productivity rates;

- salary terms and conditions;

- pricing policies;

- market share;

- image/reputation.

This type of information will not normally be available from one specific source. A range of information-gathering will need to be undertaken utilising company databases, publicly available information, newspapers, etc.

Following the completion of the internal assessment and the external review it will then be possible to undertake a SWOT analysis (strengths, weaknesses, opportunities, threats). The internal assessment will allow identification of the strengths and weaknesses of the current organisation, and the external assessment will allow identification of the opportunities that may be available and the threats to the business. The SWOT analysis should ask some key questions including:

- where can we be competitive?

- what are our unique selling points?

- which services do we want to provide and how?

- where do the opportunities lie?

- how can we manage the competition?

- what can we do about our weaknesses?

- where do we need to develop and change?

Answers to these questions will assist in developing strategic aims and objectives and subsequently the action plan.

Strategic aims and objectives

The purpose of this section is to identify the strategic way forward in order that the action plan can be developed. This will be done primarily using SWOT analysis. The first task in this section of the business plan is to document the core values and 'mission' of the organisation. Following this, the objectives behind the provision of the services should clearly be defined to include methods of delivery, anticipated cost or price and method of accountability.

Action plan

The action plan should clearly identify what needs to be done, who will do it, how it should be done, when it should be done and how success or failure will be measured. The structure of the action plan should include:

- actions required
  - activities
  - targets/objectives
  - timescales
  - outcomes

- accountabilities
  - who does what
  - decision-making and control

- resources
  - finance/capital
  - people
  - systems
  - accommodation
  - equipment

- performance measures — activities
                       — outcomes

Key steps

In many respects the methods used to produce the business plan are as important as the final document itself. It is essential that the work is done on a team basis with individual tasks allocated to specific team members. It is also important to carefully plan and manage the process and it needs, commitment, understanding, ownership and a clear focus on the priorities. The key steps in the business planning process are

Step One   — select core business planning team;

Step Two   — determine the consultation and communication process for other staff;

Step Three — design format of the plan;

Step Four   — set timescales for development and approval of the plan;

Step Five   — allocate team responsibilities;

Step Six   — allocate resources;

Step Seven — develop the key sections of the plan;

Step Eight — review the output and amend where appropriate;

Step Nine   — secure senior management/core staff commitment;

Step Ten   — commence implementation.

Developing the likely bid

At this stage in the process the in-house team should be aware of the full market testing timetable and the likely dates for tenders to be invited. Well in advance of the tender invitation date, the in-house team should seek to establish the core members of the bid team. They will be responsible not only for developing the indicative bid but also for submitting the actual tender. The indicative bid will be based upon the business plan and the bid team will use this as their primary starting point.

The first draft of the indicative in-house bid must be prepared well in advance of the formal issue of tender documentation to bidders. Absence of the specification should not stop the process from commencing, as the in-house team have a significant advantage in already having a good understanding of the current service. Prior to the development of the likely bid, it is essential that the first draft of the business plan is available to form the framework of the indicative bid.

In compiling the initial bid estimate and indeed the formal tender, due regard must be given to the costing guidance produced as part of the market testing process. This guidance will obviously reflect both the specific systems within the respective Department and the broad guidance produced by the Treasury. In developing the likely bid a full assessment of the potential cost of the operation should be made, including, where appropriate, allowances for contingencies and surplus. The primary areas which need to be considered are:

- direct staff costs;

- staff overheads;

- management costs;

- equipment and materials;

- accommodation;

- overheads;

- support services.

On the basis of the information contained within the business plan it will be possible to commence constructing a financial model of the service on the basis of a commercial business. This will enable the in-house team to understand the commercial aspects of the business and determine the costs of each of the activities undertaken by the organisation. The model will also relate the potential revenue of each activity to its cost and enable assessment of the impact of varying volumes on business viability. It will also be useful as a management tool – following a successful bid – to enable the in-house team to assess where it is making surpluses or losses and to better understand the cost implications of decisions.

The information provided by the financial model will give the in-house-team a sound basis for developing the indicative bid and determining the potential financial viability of the operation. The activities in building the financial model and developing the indicative bid are very important and are absolutely critical to the success of the in-house team in that it requires the team to think about the services and the business. This change in perspective is essential in the competitive environment in which the in-house team will operate, as they must behave as a commercial business organisation if they are to win the tender.

Comparison with potential external tenderers

As part of the business planning process, a full assessment of potential competitors should have been made, including the development of a competitor database. This information should now be used, with more detail being acquired if necessary, to evaluate the potential performance of the in-house team against external competitors. Whilst the in-house team is unlikely to know who the actual competition will be, it is likely that a reasonable estimate can be made of the potential competitors.

Focusing on the number and type of competitors within the market place, their individual characteristics and the competitive position of the in-house team, a full assessment should be made of the comparison between the in-house team and the external competitors. This should be done on the basis of both cost and quality of performance. The key objective should be to focus on the areas where one's competitors have an advantage, in order that resources can be concentrated to overcome or offset such advantages.

The competitor database should be updated at regular intervals to take account of market developments. The type and range of private sector competitors is likely to change dramatically in the formative years of market testing. It is vital that market intelligence reflects these changes. This will ensure that the in-house unit can respond to the changing environment and remain in a strong position for subsequent market tests.

Formulation of the eventual bid

Given the satisfactory development of this model and linking it to the team's already extensive knowledge of the business as it currently operates, the team should now be well placed to prepare its bid on the most favourable and competitive basis.

6 Phase 4 — the bidding process

A danger warning

There needs to be a formalised, disciplined and water-tight ethical approach running through the whole tendering procedure. From the process of the issue of invitations to tender, and carrying-on through the briefing, amplification and information exchange, and up to the final receipt of the bids themselves, great care needs to be exercised to ensure that all potential bidders are treated fairly and equally, and that the release of information and provision of assistance is even-handed. Senior managers are particularly vulnerable here, since any lapses in the established discipline will swiftly become obvious, and the whole process could be threatened.

Issue of invitations to tender

The initial requirement in this phase is the preparation and issue of the invitation to tender and associated documents.

The contract documents will vary according to the size and complexity of the business, but as a general rule the documentation should include:

- formal invitation to tender;

- the specification;

- the conditions of the contract;

- pricing and information schedules.

The letter accompanying the invitation to tender will normally spell out such details as the timescales envisaged, any pre-set briefing conferences, and how the final bids should be returned.

Figure 6.1 The six phases of market testing

	PHASE 1 Getting started	PHASE 2 Detailed planning	PHASE 3 Specifications & tender strategy	PHASE 4 The bidding process	PHASE 5 Implementing the results	PHASE 6 Ongoing contract management
Client side activity	Set up management machinery. Make appointments to key groups. Establish outline programmes. Establish policy ground rules. Prepare action plans.	Evaluate proposed activities in more detail. Develop outline tender strategy. Provide training for key staff. Begin market analysis. Select best options for market testing. Get clearance on market test programme and outline tender strategy.	Prepare service specifications and contract documents. Continue to clarify policy ground rules. Identify potential bidders. Identify evaluation criteria. Finalise contract strategy.	Commence formal tendering process. Bidding processes and presentation of bids. Tender evaluation. Post tender negotiations. Detailed evaluation report.	Communicate results. Debrief. Establish future organisation and formalise links. Ensure contract compliance. Introduce contract regime.	Continue contract compliance. Maintain awareness of customer and market. Prepare for next competition.
In-house bid team activity		Identify in-house team. Formulate in-house team strategy.	In-house team review and analysis. Development of in house business plan.	Develop bid strategy. Submit in-house bid.	Mobilise in-house service if successful. Establish client and contractor working systems.	Manage in-house service to budget. Continue to improve performance in readiness for next competition.

→ emerging client/contractor split →

CLIENT/CONTRACTOR SPLIT IN PLACE

At this stage it is important that the documentation should be clear and meaningful —the more everyone knows what they have to do to win the business, the better the competition.

PREPARATION OF CONTRACT DOCUMENTATION – CHECKLIST

- Agree the tender strategy: contract size, scope, duration, packaging and pricing method.
- Nominate the officer to whom tenderers should address enquiries and submit tenders.
- Identify the requirements and arrangements for submitting tenders.
- Agree arrangements for site visits by tenderers.
- Establish the criteria for the acceptance of tenders.
- Specify the information and documents to be submitted by tenderers.
- Produce the Invitation to Tender document.
- Prepare and complete Conditions of Contract.
- Prepare the Tender Schedules.
- Collate the Invitation to Tender, Conditions of Contract, Specification and Tender Schedules into a set of contract documentation.
- Draft a covering letter to tenderers to accompany the contract documentation.
- Arrange for the reproduction and collation of sufficient sets of contract documents.

Information

How much information should actually be released to external bidders to enable them to make the most informed and focused bid?

This is not an easy issue. The public sector exists to perform functions on behalf of the Government — this carries with it no inalienable right to 'trade secrets'. Each Department has a responsibility to spend what is, after all, public money, in the most cost effective way. It follows then, that all necessary information should be made available. Shooting in the dark is not the best way of hitting targets, and if market testing is actually about better value for money, then Departments must trade information to reduce bidders' risk, and hence, price.

This argument could extend in some market tests to the published results of any efficiency reviews relative to the area in question — in fact anything that might assist external bidders to offer a better value for money bid.

Enabling conditions

Before exploring some of the issues related to the actual bidding process itself, there are conditions which would need to be fulfilled in order to achieve the maximum benefits from the market testing process:

- tenderers must offer a fully compliant tender against the best analysis of what a Department wants and where it is feasible. This will serve the purpose of proving that they are, in fact, capable of meeting the perceived need;

- alternative offers will often be given positive encouragement with the clear understanding that commercial confidentiality will be maintained in respect of the mooted methodology, practices and cost. This should serve to bring to the forefront the flexibility and commercial innovation necessary to take full advantage of the market testing procedures;

- as a corollary to this, Departments must clearly show that they are open to new ways of achieving goals, and are willing to incorporate the outcome of extended negotiations with tenderers, so that the working methods and costs of the winning tenderers form the basis of the contract.

INVITING TENDERS — CHECKLIST

- Decide the arrangements for tenderers to submit their tenders and agree the associated instructions with which they must comply.
- Incorporate the instructions in the invitation to tender document.
- Get the contract documentation approved by the Steering Group.
- Plan the arrangements for a tenderers' briefing session and site visit.
- Ensure that a complete set of contract documentation is collated for each tenderer and the in-house team.

INVITING TENDERS – CHECKLIST continued

- Issue the contract documentation to the select list.
- Arrange to handle enquiries and information requests from tenderers.
- Deal with any requests for clarification or information in a form that can be recorded and transmitted to all tenderers.
- Set down the basis for evaluating tenders in the contract documents.
- Provide guidance on the application of TUPE.

The next stage – visits from bidders

Following the issue of invitations to tender, contractors will clearly need to examine and analyse the business, and begin to formulate their bidding strategy. Any bidder worth their salt will have undertaken a full business analysis, a comprehensive competitor analysis, and a customer/market survey, before considering any bid.

Normally the market testing team should set up a bidders' conference soon after the issue of invitations to tender, generally held on site, for the purpose of clarifying the major issues and responding to specific enquiries. This conference would be for clarification, not negotiation.

To underline the point made earlier in this chapter, an established discipline should run through all meetings and exchanges of information connected with the tendering procedures. In this respect the market testing teams should establish and enforce any necessary discipline codes, by means of positive management.

This will apply particularly to the series of subsequent meeting with individual contractors. This is a vital phase for the external bidders – their whole bid will be based upon their assessments and analyses made over the next few days or weeks. Particularly where there are high added value services which are difficult to specify, time spent getting to know the business before bidding would be time well spent from everyone's viewpoint.

Bidders will need to form an accurate view, and in the event, show confidence in that view, in financial terms, of the business, both as it stands and as it might be reshaped. Their analyses will need to cover, at the very least:

- *product* — is the current service provider giving the customers what they want? Can I improve the product itself?

- *place* — is the business situated where it should be, in terms of customers, premises and suppliers? Quite frequently, public sector businesses are located for historical reasons rather than for business considerations;

- *pricing* — how should I pitch my pricing policies? Little help is likely to be forthcoming by examining the current pricing regimes, given the different financial structures and management systems which will apply;

- *people* — what sort of quality and expertise is there amongst the current providers staff? Can I staff the business from elsewhere, more competitively? How do the current staff see my company?

- *packaging* — how can I focus my approach in the best light, in presentational terms? How much of the essential element of change should I introduce into my bid? What advantage do I have over my competitors, and how can I bring this out?

These aspects, and many others, will be uppermost in the external bidders mind during the iterative discussion period, and the market testing team's role will be to supply all the required answers, but without showing any favour to any particular bidder.

Dealing with questions

The invitation to tender should provide tenderers with details of the arrangements for making enquiries about the tender. It is not unusual for tenderers to seek clarification or additional information and, providing that information about current costs and future budgets is not given, the client should consider all reasonable requests. However, it is important that a disciplined and consistent approach to handling enquiries is adopted to ensure that all tenderers are treated equally.

The following procedures are recommended:

- keep a record of all telephone enquiries by tenderers as well as written enquiries received;

- avoid giving answers over the telephone – provide a written response;

- set a cut-off date for enquiries of ten days before the specified date for the return of tenders. Responses can then be circulated to all tenderers before they complete their tender preparations.

It is good practice to give a single person responsibility for handling enquiries, keeping records and transmitting information to tenderers. Their name, address and contact telephone and fax numbers should be included in the invitation to tender.

The final activity in this part of the process is the formal submission of bids, in accordance with procedures already detailed in the invitation to tender letter.

The in-house bid

Before taking a closer look at the next stage, tender evaluation, what of the in-house bid team? How should they be spending their time?

At the end of the last chapter, the in-house bid team had moved forward to prepare a commercial model of the business, a model encompassing the full range of commercial dynamics, together with cost and resource implications of future decisions. Its purpose was to serve as a basis for the eventual bid, a basis upon which the team could build once the invitation to tender had revealed the full extent of the market testing package and the commercial competition.

The team must now move into the final preparation phase where it will need to pull together, and focus all its previous endeavours and assemble and sharpen the eventual bid.

There are three clear strands to the in-house bid activities leading up to the formal bid:

- assimilate and utilise all additional information which emerges during the discussions with the outside bidders;

- use the commercial model to finalise the bidding strategies;

- market and sell the team itself.

As to the first of these, it is reasonable to expect the team, despite its obvious familiarity with the current business, to play its full part in the on-site bidders conference. A good deal of fresh and valuable information will undoubtedly emerge, particularly as the actual specifications have only recently become available. If the market testing team has done its job properly, that specification will have taken on board not only what the business currently supplies, but also what the customers requirements are and how the market potential might best be harnessed. The team will then have an opportunity to see and evaluate the full possibilities for innovation and flexibility that the specification allows. In addition, and importantly, the team will be able to take a first-time view of the opposition. The bidders conference will provide an excellent opportunity not only to see the other tenderers in action, but also to take an informed look at their approach, and possible strengths and weaknesses. As the process develops, the team should be able to judge from the levels, types and focus of the information which is emerging, the sort of approaches which might be in the minds of their competitors. This in turn will be a useful input into their own bidding consideration.

Secondly, the already constructed commercial model can now be fully utilised. Now that the actual specification is available to the team, they can run through the previously established options within the model and see which are most suited to the freedoms and possible innovations of the specification, in terms of developing the business to its full potential. Similarly, now that the actual packaging of the service has been spelled out in the invitations to tender, the team can discard the options which do not meet the requirements, but can prioritise those which do.

From the work on the model, a series of possible approaches, plus full details of the range of advantages and disadvantages of each should emerge, all backed by factual evidence. As an overlay to this the team will need to examine and assess the options against the background of a number of factors, including:

- possible managerial and organisational arrangements, and how these will impact on the new business;

- the forecast effect of allowable changes in pay structures, financial regimes, accommodation standards etc;

- stated service requirements − including pricing and charging arrangements, specified standards and range, and improved quality and control procedures;

- the outcome of any customer surveys which will have indicated actual customer requirements;

- the market assessment − this should clearly have indicated whether a bid should be based primarily on survival or on growth;

- the risk factor − the risks involved if the bid is won will undoubtedly be much higher than those in the team's current environment, and learning how to manage the risks, and indeed the changes, will be a difficult matter.

The third strand involves a marketing and selling exercise on the team itself, in several areas. The situation here is that the in-house team comprising career civil servants, usually with no great industrial skills (e.g. marketing, presentation, negotiation, etc), is preparing to do battle with a number of outside competitors who will have been selected for a particular range of skills needed in selling and marketing. The in-house team, as a consequence, needs to increase its skills to as high a level as possible in order to compete, and furthermore, to visibly demonstrate to as many interested parties as possible that they represent a viable alternative to the external bids and are capable of delivering the goods.

It would be easy to conclude that since the in-house bid team has been mainly selected from within the ranks of the present providers, then it will be the popular choice within the Department to win the contract − a case of 'better the devil you know'. This need not necessarily be the case. Old rivalries and bitterness tend to surface in times like these, and conversely, the current staff − who may well have seen (or indeed been subject to) the approaches of the external competitors during various on-site visits, could well prefer the outside bidders to win − seeing them as the 'friendly predator'. Loyalties and commitment could be tested if the grass on the other side looks greener. There have already been cases where current providers staff have seen better opportunities for themselves if the in-house bid fails, and have made no secret of their feelings.

So, the first area in which the team needs to sell itself and its approach is to the staff themselves, since they will presumably be of paramount importance to the success of the venture if the bid is successful.

And what of the customers? Inevitable disappointments over the years, changing requirements or dissatisfaction with the service provided may well mean that the customer might also prefer a change in provider. Again, the team needs to convince the customer that things will change for the better − the customer review already carried out should help to provide reassurance that the team will be responsive to customers' future needs and requirements (although it would be easy to ask why the in-house supplier did not undertake such customer reviews before the business was thrown open to competition!). Further selling work may well be needed to get the customers 'on side'.

Senior management within the Department may also need to be made aware that the in-house team represents the best way forward. A most useful acquisition at this time is some sort of 'champion' for the team, at a senior level and preferably in an influential position. Such a person would need to be convinced at an early stage of the advantages of the in-house bid being successful. Clearly it would be improper for any manager within the Department to interfere with the probity and propriety of the market testing process, but there will be many occasions when a sympathetic ear or voice, might legitimately assist the team in taking forward its plans and attaining its objectives. The 'better the devil you know' argument may again work in the team's favour.

There are two problems which the in-house bid team must guard against throughout the process:

- assuming the level of service required is that which is currently provided;

- the client may question the team on ability to deliver the service if major efficiencies are planned.

In most market tests the in-house team will submit a bid which is based on a lower level of resources than currently used. In doing so, the evaluation panel will need to be convinced that this will be sufficient to deliver the service. Ideally in this situation the in-house bidder will operate at these levels prior to bid submission, both to test the assumptions and to convince the client. Failing this, the in-house team must be in a position to convince the client of its ability to deliver. This can be through:

- efficiency reviews;

- recommendations from external consultancies;

- pilot studies;

- planned rationalisations;

- changed technology.

Most importantly, for planned changes to be deliverable the work-force involved in the in-house bid should be in agreement with any productivity improvements.

In summary, by the end of this phase the in-house team will need to finalise a formal bid (or number of bids) in response to the specification set down in the invitation to tender, utilising their previously constructed commercial model in the way described, and incorporating not only their own knowledge and expertise, but also drawing upon what they know of their competitors' approaches. At the same time, they will have attempted to increase their relevant skills and to convince various interested bodies that they represent the best option available and are fully capable of delivering what their bid claims they will deliver, in an effort to give their bid the necessary credibility and impetus.

The final bid will need to be cleared at senior management level to ensure that it fulfils the necessary management, structural and financial requirements, before its finalisation and presentation to the evaluation panel.

Receipt of bids and evaluation

The responses to the invitations to tender should be handled under 'sealed bid' conditions, with the opening process conducted formally in the presence of an opening panel. This maintains the essential propriety of the market testing process.

RETURN AND RECEIPT OF TENDERS – CHECKLIST

- Appoint a custodian to record the receipt of tenders and keep them securely.
- Appoint an opening team.
- Open tenders in accordance with strict formal procedures.
- Ensure that a record is kept of all tenders and of each copy of the tender.
- Open a registered file for the contract and place in it copies of all contract and tender documentation and records of the tendering process.

Tender evaluation panel

In order to evaluate the tenders, a tender evaluation panel (sometimes called a tender board) should be formed. In some circumstances it could be the market testing team itself.

In any event the panel will need to be supported by an evaluation team which will undertake all the background analysis and investigations for the panel.

The tender panel has a distinct, one off role to play in evaluating the bids. Its work will go through five stages and may include a sixth:

- stage 1 — full familiarisation with tender documents, evaluation methodology, allocation of roles/tasks and agreement to a timetable/plan;

- stage 2 — initial assessment of bids received to get a feel for the detailed task ahead;

- stage 3 — detailed evaluation of the bids to produce a preferred bid or shortlist of preferred bids;

- stage 4 — interviews of preferred bidders and shortlisted bidders to firm up on evaluation results;

- stage 5 — preparation of full evaluation report and recommended bidder;

- stage 6 — (optional and not always needed) post tender negotiations to improve planned service supply arrangements.

The quality of work produced by the tender evaluation panel is critical to the entire market testing process. It is often the first calling-off point for external scrutineers when post-tender investigations are conducted. Membership of the evaluation panel should be selected with care and full training should be given. Needless to say the in-house bid team must not be represented on the tender evaluation panel.

Evaluation Process

The main stages in the evaluation process are shown in figure 6.2. Within these stages the primary aspects are as follows:-

- compliance check;

- technical assessment;

- financial evaluation.

The compliance check takes the form of an examination of each bidder's submission to ensure that it complies with the specified tender conditions, such as information schedules, certificates and potential alterations or qualifications. Where a particular submission does not comply, then an assessment will need to be made to determine whether the bid should be rejected at this stage or if there are only minor discrepancies allowed to proceed to the next stage. The evaluation team will therefore need to judge if the degree of failure to comply is sufficient to warrant rejection.

The technical assessment focuses on whether each bidder can meet the technical and operational requirements of the specification and contract conditions. A range of issues will need to be covered and should be related to the information supplied by the contractor. The key areas to be examined should include:

- staffing levels/experience;

- management arrangements/experience;

- company structure;

- equipment proposals;

- materials;

- location/accommodation;

- recruitment policy;

- quality systems;

- customer care;

- health and safety;

- training policy;

Figure 6.2 Key stages in the tender evaluation process

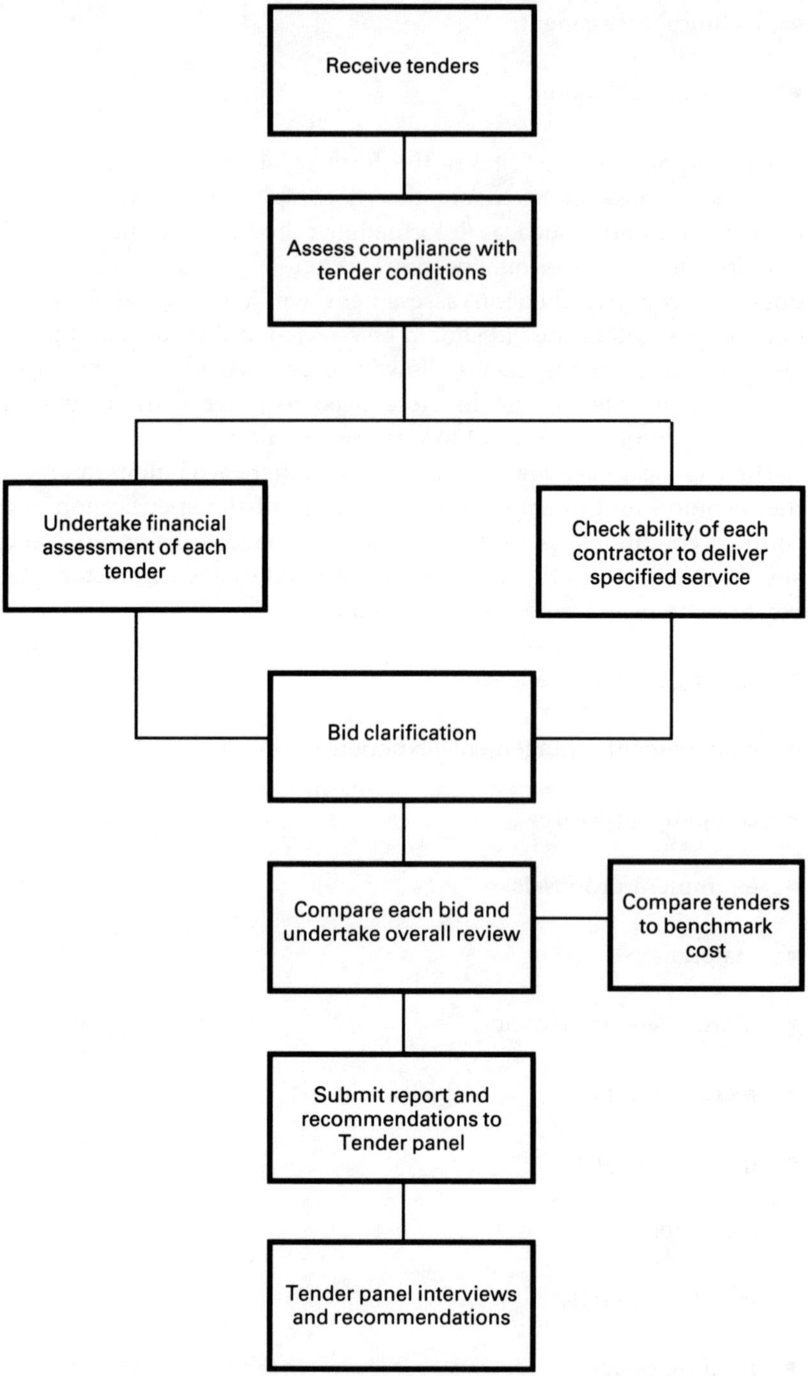

- operational plan;

- ability to deliver;

- client references;

- current commitments.

Consideration should be given to ranking contractors in key areas. In this respect it will be essential that the criteria used to judge contractor's submissions are developed in advance. This is particularly relevant where the EC Services Directive applies as the criteria must be stated in the contract documentation.

The assessment of whether a bidder can deliver the service will be based on the information submitted in his tender. However, there may be occasions when further contact is required to clarify certain issues. Any discussions must be fully documented.

The financial evaluation of bids is a complex process which cannot be treated lightly. The objective is to ensure all bids are compared on an equal basis. This may require adjustment of certain costs so that a valid comparison is made and that the full cost of the service is known. It is not a simple one-line comparison.

The detailed financial evaluation will be undertaken by the evaluation team. They should ensure that a valid comparison is made and that any adjustments are fair and equitable. Cost adjustments that may be required include those for accommodation, equipment and redundancy costs, although the latter will depend on the applicability of TUPE.

Following the detailed evaluation, an overall cost comparison will be required which also examines the current cost of the service to arrive at the full financial implications for the department.

As a result of the evaluation procedures above, it may well be that a clear winner will emerge, a tender with which the panel is well satisfied and which has a high compliance level as well as being eminently suitable in the various other important aspects. This makes life easier, but it frequently happens that several of the tenders are very close together in terms of overall acceptability, presenting the panel with a more difficult decision. In this situation, post tender negotiations may well be called for.

Post-tender negotiations (PTN)

PTN is a recognised and established practice with the basic aim of improving the value for money offered by a tendering exercise. In effect, the market testing team, having been provided by the evaluation panel with a shortlist of candidates, together with an assessment of their relevant strengths and weaknesses, may need to negotiate with each in turn.

This process is not primarily aimed at driving down costs − that would not necessarily reflect true value for money. It is more a question of an all round increase in the quality of the bid, the mutual exchange of information and an understanding of how each bid can be improved. Costs may well enter into the equation, but so too will various other factors considered important to the business. Perhaps a more efficient translation of the bidders flexibility might be sought, for instance a clarification and firming up as to how they see certain vital aspects of the business.

There are three important points which must not be overlooked during the process. First, the tendered bids would normally remain 'on the table' so that there is no risk of worse value for money emerging from the process. Second, it must be totally clear that any changes envisaged as a result of PTN do not materially alter the terms of the specification − this could mean the risk of having to re-advertise. Thirdly, the team must not run the risk of losing the best technically compliant bid by excessive use of PTN.

Clearly, the relative attractions of the various bids may alter in relation to each other during the PTN process. Experience shows that the bidders are more likely to be receptive to negotiated alterations to the original bids if the negotiator clearly has delegated authority to let and sign the contract. Personal contact and chemistry across the table counts for a good deal in these circumstances, and in commercial terms it means a lot if a bidder knows that he is dealing with someone with the authority to let the contract without further negotiations or reference upwards.

Do we include the in-house bid in PTN?

The in-house bid team are, in effect, acting on behalf of the Accounting Officer. It follows that in formulating their initial bid the team must necessarily spell out the most effective, efficient and economic arrangements that they can envisage − anything less could be construed as improper, since it would involve a degree of risk. The Accounting Officer would expect to receive, and would accept, the bid figures against this background.

There is clearly some advantage in PTN with outside contractors whose bid will normally include room for manoeuvre, in such areas as using less, or different, staff, varying investment, changing premises etc. Such room for manoeuvre should not exist in the in-house bid figures, and it would be argued that there can be no advantage in PTN with the in-house team. Indeed external bidders would regard it as anti-competitive behaviour and may seek retribution through national or EC courts.

Final recommendations

The evaluation report will formally document the decision of the Tender Panel on the award of the contract. As such it should seek to contain sufficient detail to enable any subsequent review to understand the reasons for the award of the contract to a specific tenderer. As a minimum, the evaluation report should contain:

- introduction and background to the market test;

- composition of the Tender Panel;

- contractors invited to tender;

- summary of tenders received (including prices);

- assessment of technical capability of each bidder;

- financial evaluation;

- summary of Tender Board interviews;

- Tender Board decision.

The evaluation report should be retained with the original tenders received on file. Any requests for information regarding the award of the contract by unsuccessful tenderers should be dealt with by reference to the Evaluation Report.

The benefits of structured evaluation

At the end of the evaluation, the reasoning behind eventual decisions can be explained and justified in terms of quantifiable judgments, rather than, as may have happened in the past, a vague and unmeasurable justification based as much upon personal reactions as upon focused, objectively-based evidence.

Such a factually-based explanation will be essential, given that the decision will need to be communicated in full to all parties, not just the winners (and, under EC regulations, may be formally published), and that, given the large amounts of resources involved in preparing the bids, tenderers will need to be totally satisfied with the probity and appropriateness of the process, if legal redress is not to be considered.

7 Phase 5 — implementing the results

By now the tendering process has reached its conclusion, and the decision to let the contract has been made. All too often, the time and effort required to set up and organise a soundly-based and smooth implementation is seriously under-estimated. There is still a great deal of important work to be done. For the market testing team, the following activities will be urgent:

- finalise contract discussions with successful bidder;

- inform unsuccessful bidders of the outcome;

- keep TUS/staff fully informed;

- set up the client organisation.

These activities will, in practice, be running on parallel timescales and are not set down in order of importance.

As indicated earlier in the book, the firms who have been involved in the bidding process will have invested considerable resources and money in their bids in the expectation of success. In the event of failure, those involved will be asked to explain, possibly in a rather focused and direct way, why they were not successful. Indeed, in the commercial world, their prospects of promotion, or even their actual jobs, could be on the line.

Propriety and fairness under scrutiny

As a consequence, unsuccessful bidders will inevitably examine the process very carefully in the hope of being able to cry 'foul' and perhaps, to some extent, vindicate themselves. There are two obvious areas which will fall under particularly close scrutiny in this respect, and it is here that it will become evident how well the market testing team have done their job.

Figure 7.1 The six phases of market testing

	PHASE 1 Getting started	PHASE 2 Detailed planning	PHASE 3 Specifications & tender strategy	PHASE 4 The bidding process	PHASE 5 Implementing the results	PHASE 6 Ongoing contract management
Client side activity	Set up management machinery. Make appointments to key groups. Establish outline programmes. Establish policy ground rules. Prepare action plans.	Evaluate proposed activities in more detail. Develop outline tender strategy. Provide training for key staff. Begin market analysis. Select best options for market testing. Get clearance on market test programme and outline tender strategy.	Prepare service specifications and contract documents. Continue to clarify policy ground rules. Identify potential bidders. Identify evaluation criteria. Finalise contract strategy.	Commence formal tendering process. Bidding processes and presentation of bids. Tender evaluation. Post tender negotiations. Detailed evaluation report.	Communicate results. Debrief. Establish future organisation and formalise links. Ensure contract compliance. Introduce contract regime.	Continue contract compliance. Maintain awareness of customer and market. Prepare for next competition.
In-house bid team activity		Identify in-house team. Formulate in-house team strategy.	In-house team review and analysis. Development of in house business plan.	Develop bid strategy. Submit in-house bid.	Mobilise in-house service if successful. Establish client and contractor working systems.	Manage in-house service to budget. Continue to improve performance in readiness for next competition.

→ emerging client/contractor split →

CLIENT/CONTRACTOR SPLIT IN PLACE

Firstly, the propriety and fairness of the tendering process. Previous chapters have expressed how important it is for the process to be seen to be even-handed at all times. Unsuccessful bidders will be looking back very carefully over the phases in the iterative discussions and bid development, in the hope of finalising some discrepancy in treatment (however minor) between the various bidders involved. Indeed, they may have identified and recorded any instances at the time, for future use.

Secondly, the published evaluation criteria and their impact on the various bids will clearly form part of any eventual decision. Chapter 6 stressed the value of quantifiable criteria — requirements which are clear, meaningful, and above all, measurable. The value of the use of a clearly-defined model dependent upon a number of quantifiable factors, together with definable levels of acceptability, cannot be overemphasised. If the evaluation criteria have been developed and utilised in this way, it becomes much more difficult to criticise the outcome with any justification. But unsuccessful bidders will be examining the evaluation process with a fine-tooth comb, looking for any sign of bias.

AWARD OF CONTRACT AND TENDERER DEBRIEFING – CHECKLIST

- Ensure approval has been obtained before awarding the contract.
- Ensure the client-side organisation is in place to manage the contract.
- Notify the successful tenderer in writing.
- Inform unsuccessful tenderers that their tender has not been accepted.
- Communicate the decision to staff and trade unions.
- Do not allow the contractor to start work until the contract has been signed.
- If the in-house team is successful, draw up a Service Level Agreement.
- Keep records of correspondence and meetings with the successful tenderer.
- After the contract has been awarded, debrief unsuccessful tenderers and record what was said.
- Document procedures for the contractor to use in delivering the service.
- Liaise with the contractor, users of the service and others associated with the activity to plan for a smooth start to the contract.
- Where the in-house bid is unsuccessful, take steps to rationalise existing resources.

So, at this phase, the value of a soundly-based and well-carried-out process becomes obvious — any discrepancies or weaknesses will be seized upon and, given the possibility of legal redress, could be very expensive for the organisation affected.

Even if the unsuccessful bidders are unable to specify particular examples, there must not be allowed to develop a feeling of unfairness or a sense that someone (be it the in-house bidder or not) has been given the inside track. If this happens future contracts will suffer in that potential bidders will not involve themselves.

Awarding the contract

External contract award

In general, formal award of the contract should be by joint signature of the final contract documents with a copy being retained by both parties. External contracts should not be awarded by letter of intent, nor should they be signed until post-tender negotiations have been concluded and the details of the contract worked out.

Internal contract award

In the event of the in-house bid team being successful, then the tasks are in some ways easier, and in others more difficult. The basic organisation perceived as necessary to run the contract will have been clearly set out during the team's preparations and bidding strategy, and there will be the in-built advantage of having staff already familiar with the business. The team will also have a clear view as to what it needs to do, and where it needs to do it, in terms of performance improvement, changes in standards, alterations to requirements etc.

On the other hand, the team are now in a commercial environment and despite their efforts in the previous stages of the process to alter their approach and thought-processes to a more commercially-orientated basis, they will, nonetheless, take some time to settle in.

In practical terms, they will have to be fully trained in commercial management skills and techniques. Negotiation, marketing skills, customer awareness, proper use of commercial financial systems, properly controlled monitoring of progress, target setting etc, will all need to be quickly learned and mastered. They will need to rapidly familiarise themselves with the new working arrangements, and somehow erase from their minds all aspects of how the business used to be run. Above all, they will have to learn to interpret and act upon signals provided as background information in the new commercial environment — such things as performance indicators, trading accounts, cost indicators, activity and resource utilisation levels. They may be familiar with some of these, but not all, and certainly not with the new urgency and importance which are now attached to them. Never before has their very livelihood depended upon their decisions, as it now will.

A service level agreement will be helpful in protecting the client's needs. It sets out the basis against which progress and performance can be measured.

Although SLAs are not legally binding, they should closely match the requirements that would have been set out in a contract with any external supplier. Particular attention should be paid to those parts of the agreement that monitor service levels and quality. The agreement should establish:

- the normal service to be provided by the in-house contractor;

- how the service will be monitored;

- the mechanisms for amending the level of service;

- how the agreement will be enforced;

- reporting procedures;

- the charging mechanism;

- client and contractor representatives.

The only substantial areas of difference from a formal contract should be with respect to procedures for legal redress, arbitration, payment methods and insurance or indemnity.

Staff transfers

This would seem the best time to examine the possibly thorny problem of staff takeovers or redundancies. It would be clear from the successful bid which levels and grades of staff the bidder has in mind, and it may well be the case that some firm views had been formed at an earlier stage in terms of actual personnel to be transferred. Alternatively, the bidder may not want any of the current staff. Either way, thought needs to be given at this stage to staff transfers, redeployments and the possible effects of TUPE (see Appendix 6).

Phasing-in

This takes the process as far as the actual signing of the contract, but what of the immediate period beyond? Whilst some relatively simple and straightforward contracts will be capable of starting up and running smoothly from day one, for the more complex areas of the business — such as IT services which go beyond the basic bureau services and reach into added value or software development activities — there are strong arguments to have a three month or even longer phasing-in period.

In these cases the contract spirit is the key and the letter is hammered out to fit. Whilst this recognises the problems and seeks to resolve them before the contract it is set in stone, it does require a further degree of trust.

This mutual trust must be carried forward from the market testing team — contractor relationships, where it is first developed and nurtured, through to client — contractor relationships, where it is vital to the success of the contract.

There is another aspect to the phasing-in period apart from the actual running of the business. As part of the market testing process, improved value for money and lower costs will be on the agenda. In some cases these savings will be attainable from day one (e.g. fewer or different staff involved; different premises) but in others it will be more of a gradual process — the value for money savings will need to be gradually phased-in over the period of the contract. This will call for interim arrangements and a forward plan, including milestones and targets.

It also seems sensible, given that the market testing team negotiated and put in place the actual contract, for them to have an ongoing involvement on a temporary and perhaps part-time basis. This will be useful in several ways. Firstly, it will help focus a market testing teams mind during the process if they are aware that they themselves will have the responsibility of actually implementing the contract, if only for a short while. Secondly, it will give market testing teams valuable hands-on experience, useful in reading back to any future market testing process they might be involved in. And thirdly, it will ease the task of managing the team's time, since the phasing-in period can be forecast and the levels of commitment to both the current and the next job can be adjusted accordingly.

TUS/staff relations

Earlier chapters of this book have stressed the importance of maintaining good TUS and staff relations. At no stage will the maintenance of these good relations be more important than now.

Although TUS and interested staff should have been kept in the picture as far as the earlier phases of the exercise were concerned, and whilst they will be aware that certain parts of their organisation have been subject to competitive tendering, they will not yet be aware of the initial outcome of that competition, or how it might affect them.

Once again, livelihoods will be seen as being at stake and feelings will inevitably run high. The result of the competition, after all, could be that if an external bidder is successful, large numbers of the current staff could lose their jobs or be subject to new pay structures, revised working conditions, changes in promotion procedures etc – all emotive subjects. And even if the in-house bid is successful, some, or all, of these threats could still loom large on the horizon. Extremely careful and sensitive handling will be called for, and a structured series of meetings is the best, and perhaps the only way of taking this forward satisfactorily. Senior management as well as the market testing teams should be present at these meetings, with specialist counselling readily available to cover staff fears on the personnel matters likely to be raised, e.g. redundancies. The handling will not be easy, but a degree of forward planning will make it considerably easier to handle this task than it might otherwise be.

The ramifications and interpretations of TUPE will have a considerable bearing here, and legal advice should be taken before any question of redundancies, retirements, and redeployments is formally discussed. It is also interesting to note that current instructions treat redundancies affected by Departments as if the costs were evenly spread over, say, ten years. This would seem to differ from the real world cash flow and probable contract length, and would, in effect, encourage bidders to apply a stringent 'sheep and goats' approach to any transfer of staff. This is another reason for seeking legal advice before taking action.

One final point on TUS relations. Whilst the internal TUS has a role to play in the market testing process – a fact underlined throughout this book, a further consideration comes into play once the contracts have actually been let. This is that any staff who transfer across to work for an outside contractor may well fall under the aegis of a different Trade Union and a whole new raft of agreed policies on pay, conditions, promotions etc may be applicable.

The client organisation

During earlier phases the market testing team will have put forward plans, approved by the Steering Group, for the establishment of the client organisation, that is, the management structure which will oversee the implementation and monitoring of the currently let contract, and prepare the ground for subsequent competitions.

We have now reached the stage where the client organisation should be formally set up and activated. Different contracts and businesses will call for different structures and there may well be certain minor differences in approach where the contract has been won in-house.

What is clear, however, is that the proper and efficient conduct of the client's role is essential to the Department if it is not to lose control of the contract. This will call for a clear understanding of how the new structure will function in managerial and accountability terms — understanding, not just by the client organisation itself, but also by Senior Management, the contractor, and any other Departmental staff who may have an involvement in the business.

Similarly, new structures and arrangements will need to be put in place to enable the client to exercise necessary budgeting and financial control, monitoring and restraint over the contractor. As a commercial organisation (and this will apply even if the in-house bid is successful), the objectives of the contractor are to 'manage down' costs without any perceived fall in standards. The contractor's staff will be used to this approach and to the manipulations necessary to achieve it, and the client's staff (relatively new to this game) will have to be fully aware of the possibilities.

Comprehensive and focused training would be necessary to enable the client's staff to function adequately in the way they should. They may be public servants, new to the game of commercialism, and consequently with few developed skills in the areas of overseeing commercial contracts, negotiating, marketing, and interpreting complex financial pointers. Training is a vital step for all concerned.

The end of the road?

So, we now have a contractor, a contractual arrangement, together with a client organisation in place to oversee and monitor that arrangement. In effect, the market testing process is complete, and the market testing team can move on to other fields. But that is far from the end of the story.

Control and monitoring arrangements must be put in place and these are covered in Chapter 8.

8 Phase 6 — on-going contract management

This chapter takes a look forward, now that the contract is in operation, at how the monitoring and control arrangements might be handled.

Timescale

The market testing process relies in part upon the continuous exposure to the market and competition, of activities undertaken by the public sector. In effect, if the contract is awarded for a relatively short period, then the post-implementation phase will be influenced to quite a large degree by the approaching second tender exercise. The subsequent contract, rather than the current one, will loom large in the minds of both the client and contractor — the result being that the opportunities for managing down costs and for negotiating changes will be minimal, and will be subsumed within the framework of the activities, positioning and manipulations leading up to the award of the next contract. The contractor will clearly be looking to win the subsequent contract, and his performance and approach may, therefore, not be typical during the currency of the first, short contract.

If, on the other hand, there is a longer period contract awarded initially — say for five or seven years — then the post-implementation phase will see a need to focus more clearly on tracking the evolutionary developing needs of the customer, and on monitoring the added value and value for money of the contractor as demands and conditions change.

Perhaps the most significant change to be faced is the circularity of market testing: will today's customers still be there tomorrow? If they are market tested in turn, how will the contractor and contract cope? Let's examine the practicalities of monitoring and controlling the current contract.

Figure 8.1   The six phases of market testing

	PHASE 1 Getting started	PHASE 2 Detailed planning	PHASE 3 Specifications & tender strategy	PHASE 4 The bidding process	PHASE 5 Implementing the results	PHASE 6 Ongoing contract management
Client side activity	Set up management machinery. Make appointments to key groups. Establish outline programmes. Establish policy ground rules. Prepare action plans.	Evaluate proposed activities in more detail. Develop outline tender strategy. Provide training for key staff. Begin market analysis. Select best options for market testing. Get clearance on market test programme and outline tender strategy.	Prepare service specifications and contract documents. Continue to clarify policy ground rules. Identify potential bidders. Identify evaluation criteria. Finalise contract strategy.	Commence formal tendering process. Bidding processes and presentation of bids. Tender evaluation. Post tender negotiations. Detailed evaluation report.	Communicate results. Debrief. Establish future organisation and formalise links. Ensure contract compliance. Introduce contract regime.	Continue contract compliance. Maintain awareness of customer and market. Prepare for next competition.
In-house bid team activity		Identify in-house team. Formulate in-house team strategy.	In-house team review and analysis. Development of in house business plan.	Develop bid strategy. Submit in-house bid.	Mobilise in-house service if successful. Establish client and contractor working systems.	Manage in-house service to budget. Continue to improve performance in readiness for next competition.

→ emerging client/contractor split →

CLIENT/CONTRACTOR SPLIT IN PLACE

Why do we have to monitor?

The contractor does not bid to undertake the business out of a sense of public well-being. He is not in it because he is philanthropic — he is in it, to put it bluntly, to make money. This has been clear from the outset and should not be the cause of any tensions between client and contractor.

What the client must ensure, however, is that while he is making his money, while he is taking his anticipated profits, the contractor is still complying in all respects with the terms of the contract. In other words, the standards and quality of service are not being sacrificed to improve profit margins — there is no element of managing down costs at the expense of performance.

The need for control and monitoring

Effective control and monitoring is needed to keep the contractor's performance and quality of service up to the standard specified; it is essential to assess the levels of satisfaction of customers and users of the service and areas where improvements are required, and provide clear and documented evidence to make payments to the contractor or, where necessary, any additions or deductions in accordance with the Conditions of Contract.

In addition it should anticipate and resolve any problems, provide a basis for assurances that value for money is being obtained and appraise the need for any changes in the specification or contractual arrangements at the time of re-tendering.

Organisational structure

Irrespective of the size of the contract, or whether it has been awarded externally or to an in-house contractor, the client-side must be organised effectively to manage the contract. This will normally require the appointment a client manager who, for the purposes of the contract, will be known as the Authorised Officer. A summary of typical responsibilities is given in Appendix 4. If there are a number of contracts and their value is large, the establishment of a discrete management unit should be considered.

**MONITORING CONTRACTOR PERFORMANCE —
CHECKLIST**

- Ensure agreed procedures and mechanisms are in place to control and monitor the contract.
- Confirm the responsibilities of the Authorised Officer and notify the contractor who it will be.
- Inform customers and users of the service of their responsibilities with respect to monitoring the new contractor.
- Agree with the contractor the content, format and frequency of its performance reports.
- Arrange monthly review meetings between the Authorised Officer and the contractor's manager.
- Following the start of the contract, undertake regular and random monitoring of the contractor's performance.
- Follow up customer complaints with the contractor.
- Make payments to external contractors only when the work claimed for by the contractor has been assessed and verified.
- Undertake ongoing reviews of the service levels and service standards.
- Where required, amend the contract or service specification by issuing variation orders.
- Keep comprehensive records and proper files detailing the delivery of the service and recording dealings with the contractor.
- Continuously review user satisfaction and the development of the service to prepare for the eventual competitive re-tendering of the service.

What should be monitored and how?

Contract monitoring can be divided into five aspects:

- performance — the review of contractor's performance in the delivery of services in accordance with the terms of the Specification and especially its performance targets;

- progress — the review of the timely delivery of services;

- quality — assurance of the quality of work done, through the thorough application of the processes, standards and criteria set out in the contractor's quality plan;

- propriety − scrutiny to ensure proper observance of the systems and processes, proper custody and care of equipment, proper use of accommodation and facilities, and proper qualification, experience and training of staff;

- financial − scrutiny of financial information, particularly the predicted and actual spend and commitment to future expenditure.

Relationship with the contractor

The relationship with the contractor needs to be firm but fair. It is important that inspection does not become adversarial and begin to cause conflict. No contractor can provide a satisfactory service unless their objectives, performance targets and responsibilities are clear and they receive co-operation from the organisation for which they operate. Before the contract starts, the Authorised Officer should therefore let all customers and users of the service know what they should expect from the contractor, what their role is in the monitoring process and what facilities and services the contractor will need.

Monitoring arrangements

There are effectively two methods by which services can be monitored, and they can be used together:

- by customers or users of the service, primarily by the complaints received and customer questionnaires;

- by the Authorised Officer or their support staff monitoring the services as they are performed, or afterwards.

One of the most effective ways to ensure that services are being delivered properly is to establish a system of random checks. The contractor should be informed that these will take place from time to time in addition to any regular reviews that are agreed. Any complaints from customers, users or others should also be followed up with the contractor.

While the contract is in operation, monitoring must be regular and thorough. The Authorised Officer needs to have sufficient expertise and understanding of the services to make judgements on quality and performance.

Performance reports

Contractors should be required to provide a regular performance reports covering such items as work volumes, achievement compared to the performance measures set out in the specification, complaints received from users and actions taken to rectify problems and progress in implementing any agreed changes, improvements or variations to the service.

Authorised officers should keep their own records of performance and complaints.

Review meetings

The frequency and number of review meetings will vary according to the size and complexity of the contracted service. Normally a monthly meeting between the contractor's manager and the Authorised Officer will suffice, although shorter periods may be needed if problems are occurring. In addition, a performance review meeting attended by a more senior representative of the contractor should be held every four to six months to discuss progress, problems and any necessary amendments to the contract. Where a major contract is involved, day-to-day contact between the Authorised Officer or their representative and the contractor's staff is essential.

Variation orders

Variation orders cover the following aspects:

- additions or omissions to the contract;

- changes in methods or standards;

- changes in specification clauses.

A variation order commits the client to varying the terms of the Conditions of Contract or the Specification. In most cases, issuing a variation order will mean that payments to the contractor will be revised. The revision to the price basis for the services the contractor is performing is the most important element of the variation procedure. Authorised Officers should be set a limit on the value of variation orders that they may issue. Authorisation limits should be set for single orders and for the cumulative value over the year. Variation orders should always be issued in line with the Conditions of Contract and must be authorised and signed by the Authorised Officer.

Records

Records are an essential component of the contract management process. As a minimum the Authorised Officer should ensure that records are kept of:

- correspondence with contractors and others;

- variation orders;

- minutes of meetings;

- notes of verbal discussions where there are any financial or contractual implications;

- measurements and registers of work done;

- measurements of performance taken at the regular and random reviews;

- details of complaints and problems;

- contractor's accounts as submitted, variations made and amended payments.

What differences are there if the contract is in-house?

The basic tenets of monitoring outlined above will still apply when an in-house team is awarded the contract. The same specification and service requirements will apply as to outside contractors and the

monitoring exercise will still need to ensure contract˅compliance, customer satisfaction, and maintenance of standards.

Shortfalls in performance

What happens in a case where the contractor fails to meet his contractual requirements?

There will be a continuum of possible scenarios, ranging from a minor infringement of requirements which may well be obviously a one-off with remedial action immediately promised, through to consistent, and persistent, large-scale infringements of the contract terms, possibly affecting the viability of the business as a whole. In the former case, a formal recorded warning would probably suffice, although the client would need to take particular care with the monitoring procedures over the next few weeks and months in an effort to avoid any repetition, or at least to pick up any early warning signs of recurrent problems.

As to the latter case, it would clearly depend upon how the scale and level of infringements had progressed, and how the future relationships with the contractor were viewed. The invocation of penalty clauses might have the desired effect, but in the last resort it may well be necessary to set in train legal action leading to termination of contracts, with financial recompense.

The end of the contract

The market testing process relies for its effectiveness upon continuous exposure to competition. At the end of the first specified contract, how does one proceed? Quite simply, the whole process starts all over again. Having been through the mill once, of course, certain parts of the process may be a little less time and resource-consuming, but the whole range of activities essential to good market testing still have to be undertaken. Care still needs to be exercised to show that the possibly changing needs of customers are still being catered for, and indeed, increased value for money may be required by Departments in the second round.

Where the initial contract went to an external bidder, the in-house bid facilities need to be re-examined and resuscitated. This may appear to be a large and questionable task but is well worthwhile. The in-house bid always provides a very strong price regulatory role. The private sector is always conscious of the fact that the one bid it has to beat is that of the in-house team. Consequently, there is a tendency for lower prices when an in-house bid is expected. Experience shows that price can be between 8–15% higher when an in-house bid is not to be submitted. Similarly, where the initial contract is held in-house, then the team cannot afford any complacency and needs to re-examine its whole structure and strategies.

Appendix 1: Glossary of terms commonly used in market testing

Alternative proposal
A tender from a potential contractor that proposes to deliver the service in a different way to that requested in the specification. Alternative proposals are normally only considered if they are additional to a tender which complies with the Specification and Conditions of Contract.

Authorised officer
The person who formally represents the client, deals with a contractor and has responsibility for controlling and monitoring the contract.

Base cost
The cost of the existing or current service.

Benchmark cost
The adjusted cost of the in-house bid following evaluation of tenders.

Bid
Tender submission from external or internal bidders.

Client
The management unit that procures on behalf of the users the services that are being market tested.

Collusion
Fraudulent agreements or understandings which negate the tendering process.

Competitive tendering
The process of seeking a number of competing tenders for the provision of goods or services and awarding a contract to the bidder offering the best value for money.

Conditions of Contract
The document which defines the terms and conditions of the contract. It forms part of the contract documentation.

Contract
The legal agreement between the provider of the service and the Employer paying for the service, setting out the requirements and obligations of each party.

Contract documentation
The Invitation to Tender, Conditions of Contract, Specification and Tender Schedules are the four components of contract documentation.

Contract manager
The person appointed by the contractor to be responsible for the operation of the contract to provide services.

Contracting-out
The process of engaging a contractor to perform work previously done internally. This work may sometimes be done on the contractor's own premises.

Contractor
The provider, or potential provider, of services that are being market tested. The contractor may be either an external firm which has won the work in a competitive tender or an internal operation which has been successful in the market testing process.

Contractor side
The provider side of the contract.

Customer
The management unit to whom services are provided.

DCF
Discounted cash flow analysis.

DSO
Direct Service Organisation.

EC GATT
EC developed rules which govern the procurement process of many market tests.

Employer
A contractual term defining the client-side party to the contract for the services.

Evaluation criteria
Pre determined criteria used to evaluate bids on a fair basis.

Indicative pricing
In-house bid team attempt to predict 'market' price for market tested services.

In-house bid team
Internal team created to bid in competition against private sector.

Invitation to tender (ITT)
The document which sets out the arrangements and procedures that contractors must observe in order to submit a valid tender. Also known as the *tender conditions*.

Joint venture
A collaboration between private sector bidders or internal/external bidders for the purpose of submitting a tender.

Market analysis
Assessment of market players and market conditions in any market test.

Market testing
The exercise which compares the cost and quality of operations performed in-house with what the private sector can offer and places a contract for the service with the internal or external organisation offering the best value for money.

NPV
Nett present value calculations.

Overheads
Costs added into a tender bid to account for overhead support costs.

Post-tender evaluation
The evaluation of the tender bids received from contractors to determine who should be awarded the contract.

Pre-tender evaluation
An activity that is undertaken in the initial phases of the tendering process and focuses on the selection of contractors who will be invited to bid for the contract (known as the *select list*). This process is sometimes described as *pre-qualification*.

PTN
Post-tender negotiations.

Qualified offers
A bid in which the tenderer has modified the Conditions of Contract, by proposing an amendment or substituting its own terms and conditions. This may be tendered as an alternative offer.

Qualifying the market
Shortlisting process to produce a list of potential bidders.

Service costs
The total cost of providing a service that is being market tested. For services provided in-house this includes the cost of support services, management and non-cash costs, as well as direct costs.

Service level
The breadth of services required by customers from the service provider.

Service level agreement (SLA)
A formal agreement between two in-house organizations setting out detailed task requirements, budget and criteria against which per-formance of the activity can be measured. SLAs are the equivalent of a contract when they are created following a successful in-house bid.

Service profile
A detailed description of the service being market tested e.g., describ-ing customers, outputs, resources employed, performance standards, etc.

Service users
The individuals who request and receive services from the contractor.

Specification
The document which describes the precise requirement for the services to be provided by the contractor to users of the service.

Sub-contracting
The process of letting part of a contract or activity to a third party.

Tender
The proposal from a potential contractor to provide services, made in response to an invitation from the contracting authority. It contains a bid price and normally a description of the how the services will be provided by the potential contractor.

Tender evaluation board
Teams brought together to evaluate bids and come up with a recommended choice.

Tender Schedules
A document which specifies the information and format in which tenderers are required to present their bid in order to submit a full and valid tender.

Tenderer
A potential contractor who has been invited to submit a tender to provide the services that are being market tested.

Tender strategy
The way that services are offered to potential bidders. Formulating a tender strategy, includes consideration of the size, scope and duration of the contract, and the price basis of tenders.

TUPE
The Transfer of Undertakings (Protection of Employment) regulations 1981. This legislation concerns the terms and conditions of employment for employees who are transferred as part of an undertaking.

Value for money
A concept which takes into account financial and qualitative aspects of a tender bid.

Variation order

A formal notice to the contractor of a change to the Specification or Conditions of Contract. Issuing a variation order usually means that payments to the contractor will be revised.

Vendor rating

A process to evaluate the fitness of organisations to be included on tender lists.

Appendix 2: Draft terms of reference for market testing teams

- To plan, oversee, manage, and implement the market testing process for specific activities agreed by top management, working to agreed objectives and targets.

- To undertake and develop any necessary reviews, analyses and surveys within the life of the process.

- To determine, scope and package the specific area to be subjected to market testing.

- To plan and specify future client management organisational arrangements including structure, resource requirements, costings, accountabilities and responsibilities, and the establishment of any relevant information systems.

- To establish and ensure continued effectiveness of information exchange systems, to maintain fairness and propriety.

- To prepare and draft statement of requirements and specification.

- To identify, using pre-qualification and select tender procedures where required, a list of potential contractors.

- To prepare tender documents, invitations to tender, any necessary background papers and contracts. To host tender conferences and meetings.

- To carry out tender evaluations, using pre-determined criteria, and post-tender negotiations, and to recommend the letting of contracts.

- To establish phasing-in and initial implementation arrangements, and to ensure orderly and properly phased handover to selected contractor, liaising with client organisation where necessary.

- To set up, maintain and develop good working relationships with all those involved in the process, including staff and TUS.

Appendix 3: Types of contract suitable for market testing

Given the wide range and type of service which market testing now covers, a number of different contract approaches are possible. Which one is the most suitable, or indeed whether a mix of several is most appropriate, will depend upon the specific circumstances.

The main types are:

Unit cost
This type of contract is used where the outputs can be accurately measured and agreed. The contract defines the work required and the contractor is paid for the agreed quantity of work performed. Contracts can be for the provision of labour only and materials, or whole service. The contract can be on the basis of a known volume of work (known as a bill of quantities) or alternatively with unit prices without any specified quantities (sometimes known as a call-off or measured term contract).

Lump sum
This arrangement consists of a fixed lump sum payment for work completed in accordance with an agreed, broad specification of the work/service required.

Management fee
Under this type of contract, management skills and expertise are purchased in various ways, to assist in the effective running of an existing, or planned service, generally involving in-house staff. These arrangements can be set in train in virtually any managerial set-up, although good performance indicators and realistically-based targets will generally be necessary to ensure effectiveness.

Fixed period appointments
These arrangements provide for the temporary filling by a person outside the organisation of a post which is normally already in existence but which, for various reasons (e.g. skills shortages, peaks

and troughs of work), the organisation cannot itself fill. Again, performance indicators and output measures will generally be involved to ensure that the appointee is operating well.

Incentive

This type of contract can be a development of any of the others, with the built-in addition that success, measured by whatever standards are agreed, brings with it some form of additional bonus. Conversely, failure will normally carry with it a penalty.

Retainer

A retainer contract would normally be relevant only where complex or expert advice will be needed from time to time, and where mutual confidence and trust had already been established.

Appendix 4: Responsibilities of an authorised officer

- Liaising with customers and users of the service and acting as the point of contact with the contractor.

- Meeting regularly with the contractor's manager to review the provision of services.

- Ensuring that payments claimed by the contractor accurately reflect the services actually provided.

- Certifying payments to be made to the contractor.

- Checking that service standards are maintained and that the operation is effective.

- Monitoring customer satisfaction and giving feedback to the contractor.

- Making sure that all necessary working arrangements are satisfactory.

- Co-ordinating the collection and reporting of management information.

- Managing the finance and administration of the contract.

- Assessing of budgets.

- Agreeing variations in the contract with the contractor.

- Assessing the services and the value for money obtained with a view to re-tendering when the contract period expires.

Appendix 5: Public procurement law and market testing

Prepared by Hamish R. Sandison

TABLE OF CONTENTS

1 INTRODUCTION

1.1 *Scope of the Paper*

The purpose of this paper is to provide a general overview of the current procurement law framework within which public bodies in England and Wales engage in market testing activities. Three main topics are covered:

- Part I outlines in summary form the patchwork quilt of EC rules and UK regulations (existing and proposed) covering the entire field of public procurement, including supplies, works, and services, and considers which procurement regime applies to market testing;

- Part II describes in greater detail the rules relating specifically to market testing of public services by central and local government, concentrating on the EC Services Directive and the UK Regulations implementing it;

- Part III provides an introduction to the principal enforcement mechanisms available to aggrieved suppliers at the UK and the EC level.

1.2   Local Government

In addition to the legal requirements already mentioned, market testing by local authorities in England and Wales is subject to the Local Government Act 1988. The 1988 Act deserves a seminar to itself, and is beyond the scope of the present paper.

1.3   The Law of Scotland and Northern Ireland

This paper refers only to the law of England and Wales; it does not cover the law of Scotland or Northern Ireland. As far as the EC requirements are concerned, and the UK Regulations implementing them, this makes no difference, since they apply to the United Kingdom as a whole. As far as enforcement is concerned, there are minor differences, especially in relation to remedies. In the main, however, it is safe to assume that the general principles of public procurement law are equally applicable to Scotland and Northern Ireland.

1.4   Additional Information

Official guidance to current EC rules on public procurement is contained in the EC Commission's "Guide to the Community Rules on Open Government Procurement," Notice Number 87/C358/01, OJ Number C358/1 (31.12.87), its so-called "Vade Mecum". However, the Vade Mecum is now somewhat out of date. A more recent guide, published by the DTI, IS "The Single Market: A Guide to Public Purchasing" (5th Edition March 1992). This includes information on proposed as well as current EC directives, but it does not cover the new UK regulations. The Public Competition and Purchasing Unit of

HM Treasury also publishes a number of guidance notes on public procurement, of which the most relevant to market testing is No. 34 entitled "Market Testing and Buying In".

PART I: APPLICATION OF EC PROCUREMENT LAW

2 INTRODUCTION

2.1 The EC Directives

Public procurement law at the EC level now comprises a complex patchwork quilt of interlocking Directives which have been − or soon will be − applied to cover virtually every type of public procurement activity, including supplies, works and services in the public sector and the utilities sector. This patchwork quilt is illustrated in the table attached as Appendix A.

2.2 Which Directive Applies?

In order to determine which Directive applies, it is necessary to look at:

- the nature of the contracting authority;

- the type of contract; and

- the value of the contract (or series of related contracts).

3 MARKET TESTING AND EC PROCUREMENT LAW

3.1 What is "Market Testing"?

The "market testing" activities currently being carried out by Central Government involve testing the market for the provision of certain specified services previously performed in-house. See *The Citizens Charter, First Report: 1992* (Cm2101) at pages 60–64. Similar market testing activities are being pursued by local government.

3.2   Third-Party Bids

Where market testing results in offers being invited from third-party suppliers for the provision of services to Central Government, it is clear that the EC Services Directive will apply from 1 July 1993. The EC Services Directive will also apply to local government under similar circumstances. This is because both of the general criteria for the application of the Directive are met:

- the contracting authorities are part of central or local government; and

- the procurement is for services.

Of course, whether a particular contract (or series of related contracts) is covered will also depend on whether its (or their) estimated value exceeds the relevant financial threshold.

3.3   In-house Bids

The EC Services Directive does not apply to in-house bids which are sought from units within the contracting authority. This is because the potential service provider is not a separate legal entity. Nonetheless, the Treasury Note accompanying the draft UK Regulations implementing the EC Services Directive makes clear that such in-house bids must be evaluated on the same basis as external bids from third-party suppliers.

3.4   Other Market Testing Activities

In theory, similar market testing techniques could be employed in the utilities sector in the public sector, and they could include works or even supplies as well as services. At the moment, however, the main thrust of the Government's market testing initiative involves public sector services, and so the rest of this paper concentrates on the application of the EC Services Directive and the UK Regulations implementing that Directive.

PART II: PUBLIC SERVICES CONTRACTS

4 SOURCES OF LAW

4.1 UK Regulations

The draft UK Public Services Contracts Regulations 1993 ("the UK Regulations") are intended to enact in its entirety, and without change, the EC Services Directive, as well as those provisions of the EC Compliance Directive with relate to the enforcement of EC Services Directive. Unfortunately, however, this does not mean that the UK Regulations contain an exhaustive restatement of the legal obligations of public bodies engaged in the procurement of services.

In the first place, it may be necessary to refer to the EC Services Directive itself (as interpreted by the European Court of Justice and the EC Commission) as a guide to the interpretation of the UK Regulations. In the event of any conflict or inconsistency between the provisions of the UK Regulations and the provisions of the EC Services Directive, it is the EC Services Directive which will prevail. Furthermore, the provisions of the Treaty of Rome will prevail over the provisions of the EC Services Directive and the UK Regulations, so that a public procurement decision which violates the Treaty of Rome may be considered illegal as a matter of EC law even if it does not violate the EC Services Directive or the UK Regulations.

The EC Services Directive requires that the UK Regulations came into force on 1 July 1993. This did not occur. A draft of the UK Regulations was released for consultation by HM Treasury on 3 June 1993. At the time of writing this paper the final text has not been published, and it may contain minor changes. The paper has been written on the basis of the 3 June 1993 draft.

4.2 EC Services Directive

The EC Services Directive was adopted on 18 June 1992, and the full text of the Directive was published in the Official Journal of the European Communities on 24 July 1992 (OJ No. L 209/1). The Directive must be implemented into national law by 1 July 1993.

5 FUNDAMENTAL PRINCIPLES OF EC PROCUREMENT LAW

5.1 Free Movement of Services

The underlying legal basis for the EC Services Directive is found in Article 59 of the Treaty of Rome, which prohibits restrictions on the free movement of services. The fundamental objective behind the Directive is to enhance the free movement of services in the public purchasing sector by ensuring non-discriminatory treatment of competing service providers: the provisions of the Directive (and the new UK Regulations implementing it) must be interpreted in the light of that fundamental objective, and any government action which frustrates that objective must be considered suspect.

5.2 Violation of Treaty Provisions

Public procurement decisions which violate Article 59 and other provisions of the Treaty of Rome are subject to challenge in the European Court of Justice by the EC Commission or by another Member State. For example, in *Commission v Italy (Re Data Processing)* (Case 3/88) [1989] ECR 4035, the European Court of Justice held that Italy violated not only Article 59 but also Article 52 (prohibiting restrictions on freedom of establishment) and the EC Supplies Directive by enacting decrees which specified that only companies in which all or a majority of the shares were directly or indirectly in public ownership could conclude agreements for the development of data processing systems for public authorities.

Indeed, a public procurement decision which violates the Treaty of Rome can be subject to challenge even though the decision does not violate the terms of a particular directive. For example, in *Commission v Ireland (Dundalk)* (Case 45/87) [1988] ECR 4929, it was found that the Public Works Directive was inapplicable to water distribution services, but the Court still held that Ireland violated Article 30 of the Treaty of Rome (prohibiting restrictions in the free movement of goods) by allowing inclusion in a contract specification for a water distribution contract of a clause stipulating a national standard for certain materials.

This lesson is underscored by the Treasury Note accompanying the draft UK Regulations, which warns that:

"All public bodies have obligations under the EEC Treaty with regard to the freedom of establishment of EC service providers and their freedom to provide services anywhere in the EC. Unless there is a derogation in the Treaty, these obligations extend to services specified in Part B of Schedule 1 as well as those to which the Regulations do not apply for other reasons."

6   COVERAGE

6.1   In General

Subject to certain exclusions (see paragraph 6.6 below), the UK Regulations as drafted − like the EC Services Directive − apply whenever a "contracting authority" (see paragraph 6.2 below) seeks offers in relation to a proposed "public services contract" (see paragraph 6.3 below) where the estimated value of the contract at the relevant time equals or exceeds the relevant financial threshold (see paragraph 6.4 below). See UK Regulation 5; EC Directive Article 3.

6.2   Contracting Authorities

"Contracting authorities" are defined in the draft UK Regulations to include virtually every part of central, regional and local government in the United Kingdom as well as certain quasi-governmental bodies. See UK Regulation 3; EC Directive Article 1(b).

6.3   Public Services Contracts

6.3.1   Definition

A "public services contract" is defined in the draft UK Regulations as "a contract in writing for consideration (whatever the nature of the consideration) under which a contracting authority engages a person to provide services other than:

(a)   a contract of employment;

(b)   a public works contract within the meaning of the Public Works Contracts Regulations 1991;

(c)   a public supply contract within the meaning of the Public Supply Contracts Regulations 1991; or

(d) a contract to provide services to the public which the contracting authority would otherwise have to provide and under which the consideration given by the contracting authority consists of or includes the right to charge the public for the services". See UK Regulation 2(1) (definition of "public services contracts"); EC Directive Article 1(a).

6.3.2 Contracts for Products and Services
Where a contract includes both products and services, the contract will be considered a public services contract where the value of the services exceeds the value of the supply, siting and installation of the goods. See UK Regulation 33; EC Directive Article 2. In other words, the services regime and the supplies regime are intended to be mutually exclusive, so that no contract can be subject to more than one set of Regulations.

6.3.3 Software
Difficult questions will remain, however, as to which public procurement regime applies to the treatment of software. In the supplies context, the CCTA takes the view that the suply of "off-the-shelf" software is a supply of goods; that the development of "specially written software" on its own is a service; and that the "tailoring" of an off-the-shelf product is to be treated as a service where the value of the tailoring exceeds the value of the off-the-shelf product and as a suppy if the value of the off-the-shelf product exceeds the value of the tailoring. See CCTA, *Information Technology (IT) Circular No. 328*, at page 11. The same analysis will be applicable under the new services regime.

6.3.4 Two Tiers of Services
The draft UK Regulations and the EC Directive divide public service contracts into two tiers or categories, to which different obligations apply:

- Part A services, to which the requirements apply in full; and

- Part B services, which are subject only to the requirements on technical specifications, contract award information and reports to the Commission. See UK Regulation 5(1) and Schedule 1 (Parts A and B); EC Directive Articles 8 and 9.

Public service contracts which include both Part A services and Part B services are treated as contracts for Part A services if the value of the Part A services exceeds the value of the Part B services. See UK Regulation 5(2); EC Directive Article 10.

6.4 Financial Thresholds

The minimum financial threshold for the estimated value of a public services contract for which offers are sought by a contracting authority is set at 200,000 ECU. See UK Regulation 7(1); EC Directive Article 7(1). Under Article 7(8) of the EC Services Directive, this threshold is to be converted into national currencies every 2 years with effect from 1 January 1994. The current value of 200,000 ECU for the two-year period beginning 1 January 1992 is £141,431. See OJ No. C321/6 (12.12.91). The value of a contract is to be determined at the time when a notice of the proposed procurement is due to be published in the Official Journal of the European Communities. See UK Regulation 7(12).

6.5 Avoidance Schemes

The draft UK Regulations, like the EC Services Directive itself, spell out detailed rules governing the basis for estimating the value of a public supply contract. See UK Regulation 7(3)–(10); EC Directive Article 7(2)–(7). The fundamental principle is that a contracting authority must not enter into separate public supply contracts, nor choose a valuation method, with the intention of avoiding the application of its legal obligations. See UK Regulation 7(11): EC Directive Article 7(3). Different valuation methods are specified for different types of contract. For example:

(a) In the case of a contract for the provision of services over an indefinite period, or for a period exceeding 4 years, the estimated value of the contract is deemed to be its monthly value multiplied by 48. See UK Regulation 7(9); EC Directive Article 7(5).

(b) In the case of two or more public services contracts for services of a particular type, the estimated value of each contract is taken to be the aggregate value of all the contracts. See UK Regulation 7(4); EC Directive Article 7(4).

(c) Where a contracting authority has a requirement over a period for services of a certain type, and enters into a series of contracts, or a renewable contract, for services of that type, the estimated value is to be calculated either:

(i) by taking the aggregate value of such contracts over the previous year (adjusted to take account of anticipated changes in quantity or value over the subsequent year); or

(ii) by estimating the aggregate value of such contracts over the coming year or over the entire duration of the contract (where the contract is for a definite term of more than 12 months). See UK Regulation 7(6)–(7); EC Directive Article 7(6).

However, where the services to be purchased under a public services contract are required for the sole purposes of a discrete operational unit within a larger organisation, these "aggregation" rules may be applied only to the contracts for which offers are sought by that unit. See UK Regulation 7(8). This last rule has no express counterpart in the EC Services Directive.

(d) In the case of public services contracts with option clauses, the estimated value must be determined by calculating the highest possible amount which is payable under the contract, inclusive of the option clauses. See UK Regulation 7(10); EC Directive Article 7(7).

6.6 General Exclusions

Neither the draft UK Regulations nor the EC Services Directive apply to services contracts in the utilities sector. See UK Regulation 6(a); EC Directive Article 6. As already noted, it is intended that the regulation of services contracts in the public sector and in the utilities sector should be mutually exclusive; a separate Directive to govern services contracts in the Utilities Sector has been proposed and is expected to be implemented in mid-1994. See EC Services (Utilities) Directive (COM(91) 347). The draft UK Regulations and the EC Services Directive contain a number of other general exclusions, including:

- contracts for the acquisition of land;

- contracts for the acquisition, development, production or co-production of radio or television programming;

- contracts for voice telephony, telex, radio-telephony, paging or satellite services;

- contracts for arbitration or conciliation services;

- contracts for financial services in connection with securities trading;

- contracts for central banking services;

- contracts which are classified as secret, are accompanied by special security measures, or are for the protection of national security;

- certain international contracts. See UK Regulation 6; EC Directive Articles 4, 5 and 6.

7 TECHNICAL SPECIFICATIONS

The UK Regulations and the EC Services Directive contain detailed rules governing the type of technical specifications to which reference is permitted in defining the technical characteristics of the required service, including its level of quality, performance, safety and dimensions. See UK Regulation 8; EC Directive Article 14 and Annex II. The general rule is that, wherever possible, such specifications should be defined by reference to European standards. See UK Regulation 8(3); EC Directive Article 14(2). Departures from this general rule are permitted only under narrowly defined circumstances (see UK Regulation 8(4) and EC Directive Article 14(3)), and the reasons for doing so must wherever possible be published in the OJEC notice and provided, on request, to the EC Commission or any Member State (see UK Regulation 8(6) and EC Directive 14(4)). However, other standards − including British standards − may be used in the absence of European standards. See UK Regulation 8(7); EC Directive Article 14(5).

8 PROCEDURES

8.1 *In General*

The draft UK Regulations, like the EC Services Directive, lay down three different types of procurement procedure; (a) open procedures; (2) restricted procedures; and (3) negotiated procedures. See UK Regulation 10(1); EC Directive Article 11(1). These procedures are defined in the UK Regulations as follows:

(1) **"Open procedure"** means "a procedure leading to the award of a contract whereby all interested persons may tender for the contract";

(2) **"Restricted procedure"** means "a procedure leading to the award of a contract whereby only persons selected by the contracting authority may submit tenders for the contract"; and

(3) **"Negotiated procedure"** means "a procedure leading to the award of a contract whereby the contracting authority negotiates the terms of the contract with one or more persons selected by it. "UK Regulation 2(1); EC Directive Article 1;

8.2 Choice of Procedures

Contracting authorities may use the negotiated procedure only under specified circumstances; in all other circumstances, contracting authorities must use either the open or the restricted procedure. See UK Regulation 10(6); EC Directive Article 11(4).

Contracting authorities are free to choose between the restricted or open procedures. Generally speaking, however, the restricted procedure is preferred by contracting authorities in the United Kingdom for more complex procurements; the open procedure is rarely used except for simple procurements.

8.3 Negotiated Procedure

The negotiated procedure is permitted only under limited circumstances. See UK Regulation 10(2); EC Directive Article 11(2) and 11(3). It may be used with prior publication of a contract notice in the following three cases:

(1) where an open or restricted procedure was discontinued because of "irregular tenders", *i.e.*, tenders which failed to meet the contracting authority's requirements (see UK Regulation 10(2)(a) and EC Directive Article 11(2)(a));

(2) in exceptional cases when the nature of the services or their risks are not such as to permit "prior overall pricing" (see UK Regulation 10(2)(b) and EC Directive Article 11(2)(b)); and

(3) when the nature of the services is such that specifications cannot be drawn up "with sufficient precision to permit the award of a

contract using the open or the restricted procedures", for example in the case of what the Directive calls "intellectual services" and the UK Regulations call "a service involving conceptual thought" or in the case of financial services.

The negotiated procedure may also be used without prior publication of a contract notice in the following circumstances:

(1) In the absence of appropriate tenders or any tenders in response to an ITT by the contracting authority using the open or restricted procedure (see UK Regulation 10(2)(d)) EC Directive Article 11(3)(a));

(2) when, for technical or artistic reasons, or for reasons connected with the protection of exclusive rights, the services may be provided only by a particular person (see UK Regulation 10(2)(e); EC Directive Article 11(3)(b);

(3) when the rules of a design contest require the contract to be awarded to the successful contestant or to one of the successful contestants, provided that all successful contestants are selected to negotiate the contract (see UK Regulation 10(2)(f); EC Directive Article 11(3)(c));

(4) when for reasons of extreme urgency brought about by events unforeseeable by, and not attributable to, the contracting authority, the relevant time limits cannot be met (see UK Regulation 10(2)(g); EC Directive Article 11(3)(d));

(5) for additional services which were not originally included in the project through unforseen circumstances and which either cannot without great inconvenience to the contracting authority be provided separately for technical or economic reasons, or are strictly necessary for the completion of the contract, although in either case the aggregate estimated value of contracts awarded for additional services may not exceed 50% of the value of the original contract (see UK Regulation 10(2)(h); EC Directive Article 11(3)(e));

(6) for new services which are repetition of services provided under the original contract and which are in accordance with the project for which the main contract was entered into, provided that this possibility was so stated in the OJEC notice relating to

the original contract, and the procedure for the award of the new contract is commenced within 3 years of the original contract (see UK Regulation 10(2)(i); EC Directive Article 11(3)9f)).

8.4 Time Limits

The UK Regulations and the EC Services Directive lay down time limits for certain events in the open, restricted and negotiated procedures. The time limits are as follows:

(1) in the case of open procedures, the deadline for the receipt of tenders must be not less than 52 days from the date of despatch of the contract notice (or 36 days where the contracting authority has published a "prior information notice"), although these deadlines must be extended if tenders can only be submitted after a site visit (see UK Regulation 11(3), (4) and (7); EC Directive Article 18(1), (2) and (5));

(2) in the case of restricted procedures and negotiated procedures preceded by publication of a contract notice, the deadline for the receipt of requests to participate in the procurement must be not less than 37 days from the date of the dispatch of the contract notice (see UK Regulations 12(3) and 13(3); EC Directive Article 19(1)); and

(3) in the case of restricted procedures, the deadline for the receipt of tenders in response to the Invitation To Tender ("ITT") must be not less than 40 days from the dispatch of the ITT (or 26 days where the contracting authority has published a "prior information notice"), although these deadlines must be extended if tenders can only be submitted after a site visit (see UK Regulation 12(11)–(13); EC Directive Article 19(3), (4) and 19(7)).

In restricted and negotiated procedures, these time limits may be reduced to 15 days and 10 days (respectively) where urgency renders them "impracticable". See UK Regulations 12(15) and 13(4); EC Directive Article 20.

8.5 Urgency

Although urgency may be cited as a reason for reducing certain time limits, it is not generally an excuse for avoiding "restricted" (*i.e.* competitive) tendering altogether. As noted above, however, urgency may be cited as a justification for using "negotiated" (*i.e.* non-competitive) tendering insofar as it is "strictly necessary" for reasons of "extreme urgency brought about by events unforeseeable by the contracting authority". UK Regulation 10(2)(g); EC Directive Article 11(3)(d). The EC Directive, goes on to provide that "the circumstances invoked to justify extreme urgency must not in any case be attributable to the contracting authorities" (EC Directive Article 11(3)(d)), and the UK Regulations are to similar effect (see UK Regulation 10(2)(g)).

9 ADVERTISING REQUIREMENTS

9.1 In General

Nothing in the EC Services Directive or the draft UK Regulations is more critical to the accomplishment of their underlying objective – the free movement of services in the public purchasing sector – than the requirement that the proposed award of a public services contract should be advertised in OJEC: without such an advertisement, there can obviously be no possibility of ensuring equal conditions of competition for potential service providers throughout the European Community. It should be noted, however, that the advertising requirements only apply to the procurement of Part A services. See draft UK Regulations 5(2) Schedule 1A; EC Directive Article 8, Annex 1A. These requirements apply to open, restricted and (subject to the exceptions noted above) or negotiated procedures.

9.2 Prior Information Notices

Contracting authorities must advertise prior information notices in the OJEC as soon as possible after the beginning of their financial year giving details of public services contracts relating to services in Part A where:

(a) such contracts have an estimated annual value of more than 750,000 ECU (£530,366); or

(b) such contracts have an estimated value of more than 200,000 ECU (£141,431) and, after applying the aggregation rules, the estimated value of other public services contracts for the provision of the same type of service is more than 750,000 ECU (£530,366) during the relevant year. See UK Regulation 9(2); EC Directive Article 15(1).

The prior information notice must be drawn up "substantially" in a form corresponding to the model notice set out in Schedule 2, Part A, of the UK Regulations and Annexe 1A of the EC Directive.

9.3   Contract Notices

In addition to a prior information notice, contracting authorities using the open, restricted and (subject to the exceptions noted above) negotiated procedures must also advertise their intention to seek offers for public services contracts relating to Part A services by sending a contract notice to the OJEC in the prescribed form. See UK Regulations 11(2), 12(2), and 13(2); EC Directive Article 15(2). The draft UK Regulations and the EC Directive specify a model form of notice as follows:

- for open procedures, see Schedule 2 Part B of the UK Regulations and Annexe III Part B of the EC Directive;

- for restricted procedures, see Schedule 2, Part C of the UK Regulations and Annexe III Part C of the EC Directive; and

- for negotiated procedures preceded by publication of a contract notice, see Schedule 2 Part D of the UK Regulations and Annexe III Part D of the EC Directive.

The contract notice must be submitted in this form to the Official Journal of the European Communities as soon as possible after a contracting authority has formed its intention to seek offers for a public service contract. See UK Regulation 11(2), 12(2) and 13(2). The notice is not to contain more than 650 words. See UK Regulation 29(2); EC Directive Article 17(8). It should be sent to the Office for Official Publications of the European Communities, 2 Rue Mercier, 2985 Luxembourg (telephone 499 28-1; telex 1324 pubof lu; fax 490003, 495719), and should be transmitted by telex, telegram or fax where the contracting authority seeks reduced time limits for reasons of urgency. See draft UK Regulation 29(1); EC Directive Article 17(2).

The contracting authority should retain evidence of the date of despatch (see UK Regulation 29(3); EC Directive Article 17(7)), and the Official Journal must publish the notice within 12 days of despatch (see EC Directive Article 17(5)), or within 5 days where the contracting authority seeks to reduce the time limits in cases of urgency (see EC Directive Article 17(5)).

A contracting authority should not place a notice of the proposed contract in the UK press before the date when its notice is despatched to the Official Journal, and if it does publish such a notice after that date it should not add any additional information which is not contained in the notice sent to the Official Journal. See UK Regulation 29(4); EC Directive Article 17(6).

9.4   Contract Award

Contracting authorities must also submit for publication in the OJEC a notice of all contracts awarded within 48 days after their award, and a model form of notice is specified for this purpose. See UK Regulation 21(1) and Schedule 3 Part E; EC Directive Article 9(3)–(4) and Annex III Part E.

10   CRITERIA FOR SELECTION OF TENDERERS

10.1   In General

In restricted and negotiated procedures (though not of course in open procedures), contracting authorities may select from among the suppliers which have responded to the OJEC notice those which will be invited to tender or negotiate, provided that such selection is made on the basis of certain criteria to which reference permitted. See UK Reguation 12(4) (restricted procedures) and UK Regulation 13(7) (negotiated procedures); EC Directive Article 27(1). The same criteria apply to the exclusion of tenders received in open procedures. See UK Regulation 11(8). These criteria include:

- the supplier's soundness and integrity (see UK Regulation 14; EC Directive Articles 29–30;

- its economic and financial standing (see UK Regulation 15; EC Directive Article 31); and

- its technical capacity (see UK Regulation 16; EC Directive Articles 32–33).

Under no circumstances, however, may the contracting authority discriminate between suppliers on the grounds of their nationality or the member state in which they are established when selecting them to tender or negotiate. See UK Regulations 12(5) and 13(8); EC Directive Article 27(4).

10.2   Minimum Number of Competing Suppliers

In restricted procedures, the contracting authority may predetermine a fixed number of competing suppliers which will be invited to tender provided that:

(1)   the number of is not less than 5 and not more than 20;

(2)   this range is determined in the light of the nature of the services to be provided under the contract; and

(3)   the range of numbers is specified in the contract notice.

However, the number of competing suppliers must in every case be "sufficient to ensure genuine competition". See UK Regulation 12(6) and (7); EC Directive Article 7(2).

In negotiated procedures, the number selected to negotiate must be not less than three, provided that there is a sufficient number of persons who are suitable for selection to negotiate applying the criteria to which reference is permitted. See UK Regulation 13(5); EC Directive Article 27(3).

10.3   Supplementary Information

According to the draft UK Regulations, the contracting authority may require a service providers to provide supplementary information to determine its compliance with these criteria or to clarify information provided by the service providers, but only if the supplementary information relates to the specified criteria. See UK Regulation 17. However, the European Court of Justice has held that the list of criteria specified in the Directive is not exhaustive, and that reference to additional criteria is permitted, so long as such criteria are not discriminatory. See *Gebroeder Beentjes DV v State of Netherlands* (Case 31/87).

10.4   Quality Assurance

In assessing whether a supplier meets any minimum standards of technical capacity, a contracting authority is permitted to consider, among other things, whether the supplier has a certificate under BS5750 or an equivalent European quality assurance certificate. See UK Regulation 16(1)(h); EC Directive Article 33.

10.5   Official Lists

Where a supplier is registered on the official list of a member state which maintains such lists, the contracting authority must accept a certificate of registration issued by the relevant national authority as evidence that the supplier meets any criteria of soundness and integrity, economic and financial standing, and technical capacity specified in the certificate, and the contracting authority is not entitled to require the supplier to supply supplementary information already specified in the certificate. See UK Regulation 18; EC Directive Article 35.

10.6   Confidentiality

The contracting authority must comply with any confidentiality requirements reasonably requested by a service provider. See UK Regulation 30; EC Directive Article 32(4).

10.7   Consortia

The contracting authority is not permitted to exclude a tender submitted by a consortium of two or more persons on the grounds that the consortium has not formed a legal entity for the purpose of tendering. However, following the award of a contract to the consortium, the contracting authority may require the consortium to form a legal entity before entering into, or as a term of, the contract if such requirement is justified for the satisfactory performance of the contract. See UK Regulation 19(2); EC Directive Article 26(1).

10.8   Subcontractors

A contracting authority may require a supplier to indicate in its tender what part of the contract is to be subcontracted to a third party. See UK Regulation 31; EC Directive Article 25. However, the EC Directive makes clear that any proposed subcontracting need not prevent the contracting authority from requiring the supplier to assume prime contractorship responsibility. See EC Directive Article 25.

11   CRITERIA FOR AWARD OF CONTRACT

11.1   In General

The draft UK Regulations and the EC Directive provide that contracts may be awarded on the basis of one or other of the following two alternative criteria:

(a)   "lowest price"; or

(b)   the "most economically advantageous" tender. UK Regulation 21(1); EC Directive Article 36(1).

In determining whether a tender is the most economically advantageous tender, the contracting authority may use such criteria as "price, period for completion or delivery, quality, aesthetic and functional characteristics, technical merit, after sales service and technical assistance." UK Regulation 21(2); EC Directive Article 36(1).

However, there is nothing in the UK Regulations or the EC Directive to require a contracting authority to accept any tender or award any contract.

11.2   Most Economically Advantageous Tender

Where an award is to be made on the "most economically advantageous" basis, all the criteria to be applied must be stated either in the OJEC notice or in the contract documentation (such as the ITT), preferably in descending order of importance. See UK Regulation 21(3); EC Directive Article 36(2).

11.3   Abnormally Low Bids

Even where an award is to be made on the "lowest price" basis, the draft UK Regulations and the EC Directive allow contracting authorities to reject a tender which is "obviously abnormally low". UK Regulation 21(7); EC Directive Article 37. However, if a tender is rejected on this ground, the contracting authority must justify its decision to HM Treasury and ultimately the EC Commission. See UK Regulation 21(8); EC Directive Article 37.

12   OTHER REQUIREMENTS

12.1   Annual Statistical Reports

Contracting authorities in the UK must submit certain statistical reports to HM Treasury in 1995 and in odd numbered years thereafter concerning public services contracts awarded by them over the previous even numbered year (see UK Regulation 27(1)).

Other reports may be requested by HM Treasury from time to time. See UK Regulation 27(2).

12.2   De-Briefing

Contracting authorities must inform an unsuccessful tenderer within 15 days of request of the reasons why the tenderer was unsuccessful and of the name of the successful tenderer. See UK Regulations 23(1); EC Directive Article 12(1). In addition, the contracting authority must prepare a record of the procedure containing certain specified details. See UK Regulations 23(2); RC Directive Article 12(3).

PART III: ENFORCEMENT

13   INTRODUCTION

Two principal mechanisms are now available to enforce the EC Services Directive. At the domestic level, the draft UK Regulations will give aggrieved suppliers specific judicial remedies against a contracting authority which fails to comply with the new Regulations or any other enforceable EC obligation (see paragraph 17 below). At the EC level, both the EC Commission and other Member States have power to bring infringement proceedings in the European Court of Justice against a Member State which fails to implement or comply with the provisions of the EC Services Directive or the Treaty of Rome itself (see paragraph 18 below).

In addition to these actions to enforce the UK Regulations, there may also be an action for breach of an implied tendering contract where a contracting authority has failed to comply with applicable procurement law – including the UK Regulations.

14 DRAFT REGULATION 32

14.1 Introduction

The draft UK Regulations implemented into United Kingdom law the obligations of the EC Compliance Directive by introducing specific remedies which enable aggrieved service providers to enforce the provisions of the UK Regulations against non-compliant contracting authorities in the United Kingdom courts.

14.2 Who May Bring an Action?

Any service provider who suffers, or risks suffering, loss or damage as a result of any non-compliance by a contracting authority during a procurement process is entitled to bring an action against the contracting authority. See draft UK Regulation 26(2). This means that the list of possibly aggrieved service providers who are entitled to bring action against contracting authorities is very broad, ranging from the company which would have won the procurement process had it been properly conducted, through companies which consider that they were improperly excluded from the short-listing process, to companies which did not respond to the OJEC advertisement because it was improperly worded. However, only service providers which are nationals of and established in the EC are entitled to bring a court action against a contracting authority under the Regulations. See draft UK Regulation 4(1).

14.3 Procedural Requirements

Before commending an action for breach of the UK Regulations, a service provider must notice the contracting authority that it considers that a breach of the UK Regulations has occurred and that it intends to bring an action in respect of the perceived breach. See UK Regulation 32(4).

All United Kingdom court actions for breaches of the UK Regulations must be brought in the High Court in England and Wales and in the Court of Session in Scotland. The court action must be commenced promptly and, in any event, within three months of the date when the grounds for the action first arose. This means that even if the action is commenced within the three month deadline, the court could consider that excessive delay had occurred and that the action should not be heard. In very rare cases a court is entitled to give consent to an action which is commenced outside the three-month deadline. See UK Regulation 32(4).

14.4   Interim Measures

The courts are entitled to grant emergency relief prior to a final trial. The courts have the right to grand orders which:

a)   suspend the procedure leading to the award of a contract; or

b)   suspend the implementation of any decision or action taken by the contracting authority in the course of following a contract award procedure.

Hence, the courts have wide power to stop a procurement procedure in its tracks during the period up to the final trial of the issue. See UK Regulation 32(5).

The principles upon which the court may decide whether to grant an interim order will be based upon the standard principles for the grant of interlocutory injunctions. In particular, the court will:

(1)   examine whether there is a serious issue to be tried;

(2)   consider whether damages would be an adequate remedy at final trial; and

(3)   weigh up the "balance of convenience", *i.e.*, whether the applicant would suffer more damage if the order was not granted as compared with the damage that the contracting authority would suffer if the order were to be granted.

More often than not, the court will act to maintain the status quo. It is quite likely that in many cases an application by an aggrieved service provider for an interim order would be granted which would suspend the procurement procedure in order to ensure that a contract is not improperly awarded. However, where a contracting authority can establish that there is a genuine need for urgency in the implementation of the contract, the courts are liess likely to grant interim relief.

14.5   Final Remedies

The UK Regulations provide that at the final trial the courts may order the setting aside of a decision or action, or the amendment of a document, or award damages to a service provider who has suffered a loss or damage as a result of non-compliance with the UK Regulations.

However, the non-financial remedies are only available before a contract is entered into. After a contract has been entered into, the court loses the right to award any remedy other than damages. See UK Regulations 32(6). Hence, where aggrieved service providers consider that they may have an action against a contracting authority, they will need to act quickly in order to avoid losing their ability to prevent the award of a contract in breach of the law.

Damages may be awarded by the court both before and after a contract has been entered into. Damages are available to service providers and contractors who have suffered loss or damage as a consequence of the non-compliance. In contrast to the UK Utilities Regulations, the UK Services Regulations do not expressly state that a supplier which would have had a "real chance" of winning the procurement if it had been conducted properly is entitled to recover the costs of preparing its tender or participating in the procurement process. However, the courts may well award damages on this basis in any event.

Additional damages may also be available to the service provider which would have won the procurement if it had been conducted properly. These damages may include the loss of profit which the service provider would have made had it been awarded the contract. Damages may also be available for the loss of the opportunity of winning the procurement. However, the measure of damages for a loss of opportunity is rather uncertain and it is not clear that the court would regard this as a category of damages which should be available in the circumstances.

Thus, contracting authorities should note that where procurements are not conducted in accordance within the UK Regulations, damages will potentially be available to more than one aggrieved tenderer. It may well be that all tenderers which had a "real chance" of winning the procurement will be entitled to recover their tendering costs. In addition, the tenderer which should have won the procurement will also be entitled to recover its loss of profits. Therefore, contracting authorities could face claims for substantial damages if they fail to comply with the requirements of the UK Regulations.

15 ENFORCEMENT AT THE EC LEVEL

15.1 Introduction

The EC Compliance Directive sets out a procedure for the EC Commission when it wishes to enforce the provisions of the EC Services Directive. The Commission is entitled to take action to enforce the EC Services Directive when it considers that a clear and manifest infringement of the Directive has been committed. See EC Compliance Directive Article 3(1).

15.2 Administrative Stage

Before bringing proceedings in the European Court of Justice ("ECJ"), the EC Commission goes through a three-stage administrative process in an attempt to secure compliance with the relevant Directive. See Compliance Directive Article 3; Vade Mecum OJ No. C358/40–41.

- First, the Commission notifies the Member State and the contracting authority concerned of the reasons which have had led it to conclude that an infringement has occurred and requesting its correction.

- Second, the Member State has 21 days in which to respond by:

  a) confirming that the infringement has been corrected;

  b) providing a reasoned submission as to why no correction has been made; or

  c) notifying the Commission that the contract award procedure in question has been suspended either by the contracting authority or on the basis of an order of the national courts.

- Third, if the Commission is not satisfied with the Member State's response, it serves a "reasoned opinion' on the Member State ordering it to take remedial action by a certain date.

If the Member State does not comply with the Commission's reasoned opinion by that date, the Commission is entitled (but is not required) to move to the judicial stage of the enforcement process.

15.3 Judicial Stage

Having complete the administrative stage of the enforcement process, the EC Commission may commence proceedings before the ECJ against the Member State concerned under Article 169 of the Treaty of Rome. The Commission does not have power to bring actions directly against contracting authorities. It should be noted that the Commission's action before the ECJ is not subject to the three-month deadline which applies to actions by aggrieved suppliers in the domestic courts.

15.3.1 Interim Remedies

Once the action has been commenced at the ECJ, the Commission is entitled to apply for interim measures prior to the final trial of the matter. Any type of order may be made by the court as an interim measure as long as the order does not go further than is necessary to safeguard the effectiveness of the court's final judgement, and the order is temporary and provisional in nature. An order for interim measures will only be granted if it is shown that there is a need for urgency in order to avoid serious and irreparable harm and that there is a *prima facie* case to answer.

15.3.2 Final Orders

If the ECJ finds at the final trial that the Commission's case is proved, it will give judgement against the Government. This takes the form of a declaration that the relevant member state has failed to fulfil an obligation under the Treaty of Rome and sets out details of the act or omission which is the source of the infringement. The ECJ is not entitled to award damages against the Government. Following judgement, the Government is required to take the necessary measures to comply with the ECJ's judgement. This may entail action by the Government to force the relevant contracting authority to comply with the judgement of the ECJ.

16   THE IMPLIED TENDERING CONTRACT

16.1   Introduction

The English Court of Appeal has held that an Invitation To Tender
(ITT) may under certain circumstances give rise to an implied contract
between a contracting authority and all participating tenderers pur-
suant to which a conforming tender must be considered in conjunc-
tion with all other conforming tenders. See *Blackpool and Fylde Aero
Club Ltd v Blackpool Borough Council* [1990] 3 All ER 25. This decision
has far-reaching implications for public procurement law. In addition
to creating a contractual obligation to consider all conforming tenders, such an implied tendering contract might also be construed to
contain additional terms obliging the contracting authority to act in
accordance with applicable procurement law — including the new UK
Regulations and the EC Services Directive — and in accordance with
any other procedures specified in its tender documentation, whether
or not required by the EC Directive or the new UK Regulations.

16.2   The "Blackpool" Case

In the *Blackpool* case, the defendant, Blackpool Borough Council,
invited the plaintiff, the Blackpool & Fylde Aero Club Ltd, to submit
a tender for a concession to operate pleasure flights from Blackpool
airport. Six other parties were invited to tender. The ITT stated that:
"No tender which is received after the last date and time specified
shall be admitted for consideration". [1990] 3 All ER at 27. Although
the club's tender was dropped in the council's letterbox before the
specified deadline, the council's staff failed to empty the box as they
were supposed to. As a result, the club's tender was mistakenly
recorded as being late, and was excluded from consideration. When
the council decided to award the contract to another tenderer, the
club sued the council for damages, alleging a breach of contract and
negligence.

Both the trial judge and the Court of Appeal held that the council was
liable for a breach of an implied tendering contract with the club.
According to Lord Justice Bingham, such a contract arises out of the
following circumstances:

> "Where, as here, tenders are solicited from selected parties all of
> . them known to the invitor, and where a local authority's invitation

prescribes a clear, orderly and familiar procedure (draft contract conditions available for inspection and plainly not open for nego-tiation, a prescribed common form of tender, a supply of envelopes designed to preserve the absolute anonymity of tenderers and clearly to identify the tender in question and an absolute deadline) the invitee is in my judgement protected at least to this extent: if he submits a conforming tender before the deadline he is entitled, not as a matter of mere expectation but of contractual right, to be sure that his tender will after the deadline be opened and considered in conjuction with all other conforming tenders or at least that this tender will be considered if others are." [1990] 3 All ER at 30.

In reaching this conclusion, the Court of Appeal acknowledged that the council had not expressly agreed to consider all timely and conforming tenders. Such agreement could only be found by implica-tion, but the implication was justified because:

"Had the club, before tendering, enquired of the council whether it could rely on any timely and conforming tender being considered along with others, I feel quite sure that the answer would have been 'of course'. The law would, I think, be defective if it did not give effect to that." [1990] 3 All ER at 30–31.

16.3   Implications of the "Blackpool" Case

On the fact before the court, the terms of the implied tendering contract in the *Blackpool* case were quite limited: the contracting authority was held to have agreed that, if the tenderer submitted a conforming tender, it would be considered along with all other conforming tenders.

However, the implications of the decision are much more extensive. If an implied tendering contract can be found to arise whenever an ITT established a "clear, orderly and familiar procedure' for inviting tenders, such a contract will be found to exist in most public procurements. If an implied tendering contract exists, the terms of that contract may also be implied. As indicated by the court, the accepted test for implying such terms is whether one party, if asked by the other party whether it accepted a particular obligation, would have replied "of course".

Applying this test, it seems likely that contracting authorities covered by the UK Regulations or the EC Services Directive can be held to have accepted at least two additional obligations as terms of their implied tendering contracts, since their answer to the following questions from a potential tenderer must surely be "of course":

(a) Do you agree to follow the requirements of UK Regulations and the EC Services Directive?

(b) Do you agree to follow the tendering procedures specified in your OJEC notice/RFP/ITT/standing orders, etc?

It follows that, if the contracting authority violates any of these implied terms, it is liable for breach of its implied tendering contract with all participating tenderers.

16.4 Remedies for Breach of Contract

In addition to the usual non-financial remedies (such as a declaration or an injunction), damages are available to a private party who has successfully established that a contracting authority is in breach of an implied tendering contract. The purpose of damages is to compensate the plaintiff for the defendant' breach. Thus, there are two obvious ways of measuring damages for breach of an implied tendering contract:

(a) lost profits, *i.e.*, the profits the tenderer would have earned if it had been awarded the contract; or

(b) tendering costs, *i.e.*, the costs actually incurred by the tenderer in preparing its tender.

Lost profits are likely to be awarded only if the tenderer can show that it would have been awarded the contract but for the contracting authority's breach of the implied tendering contract.

A third possible way of measuring damages is to assess the value of the tenderer's lost opportunity to compete: this might be an appropriate measure of damages if the tenderer could not show that it would have won the contract but for the breach, or if it had not incurred any tendering costs before the breach. This measure of damages is not unknown to the law of contract, but it is obviously highly speculative and unlikely to yield a large award. See *Chaplin v Hicks* [1911] 2 KB 786 (CA).

Appendix 6: Personnel issues, in particular TUPE

Origin of the regulations

The Transfer of Undertakings (Protection of Employment) Regulations 1981 ("TUPE") were made to implement the European Communities' Acquired Rights Directive (EEC187/77). The purpose of TUPE and the Acquired Rights Directive is to protect employees when the business for which they work is transferred to a new employer. Both provide that:-

- the rights and obligations of the old employer and the contract of employment are automatically transferred to the new employer — except insofar as they relate to pensions;

- dismissals for reasons connected with the transfer are automatically unfair unless they are for an "economic, technical or organisational reason";

- the old employer is required to inform and consult employees about the transfer before it takes place.

- trade union recognition and collective agreements continue after the transfer (but the new employer, like the old employer, is entitled to withdraw from both);

Scope of TUPE and the Acquired Rights Directive

Because TUPE implements the United Kingdom's obligations under the Acquired Rights Directive, courts and tribunals in the United Kingdom are bound by certain decisions of the European Court of Justice on the scope and implications of the Directive. Both the

Directive and TUPE are expressed in general terms. Although it has always been clear that the Directive and TUPE apply to the sale of a business, it has only recently become clear that market testing, contracting-out services and outsourcing can constitute "transfers of undertakings" which come within their scope. The turning point was the judgment of the European Court in *Rask and Christensen v ISS Kantine Service A/S*. That decision draws heavily on earlier judgments of the Court. In Rask the European Court held that contracting out canteen services at Philips factories could come within the scope of the Directive. The Court said that the decisive criterion is whether the entity concerned retains its identity after the transfer. Thus where a contract for market testing transfers to a contractor work which is carried out after the transfer in the same place by the same people using the same machinery or equipment, it is likely that TUPE and the Regulations will apply.

Practical consequences if TUPE does apply

If they apply TUPE and the Directive will impose obligations on the market testing organisation and the contractor irrespective of their wishes. If they apply:

- the contractor will automatically become the employer of the employees who work in the service for which it becomes responsible

- the employees will be entitled to the same terms and conditions with the contractor except for pensions which are a special case (see below)

- employees who are dismissed for a reason connected with the transfer will be automatically unfairly dismissed unless it can be shown that the dismissals are for an "economic, technical or organisational reason"

- the employees' continuity of service is preserved and will continue unbroken with the contractor

- the contractor is bound to the same extent as the market testing organisation by union recognition and collective agreements

- before the transfer takes place the market testing organisation is obliged to inform and consult trade unions about changes in terms and conditions which the contractor intends to make

Issues which in practice cause most difficulty are redundancy, changing terms of conditions and pension rights

Redundancy

Where TUPE applies, the contractor takes over responsibility for the contracts of employment of all the employees who were assigned to the service which is contracted out. These employees transfer to the contractor on the same terms and conditions as they had with the market testing organisation, except in relation to pensions. Thus the employees are not redundant or entitled to redundancy compensation just because of the transfer.

It is, of course, possible that the contractor may want to make redundancies to reduce the number of employees. In this case, the redundancies may be for an "economic, technical or organisational reason". If so, the dismissals will be fair if the contractor acts reasonably. In determining this an industrial tribunal would treat the dismissals as normal redundancies and assess their fairness taking account of matters such as the procedure for selecting employees and whether the contractor gave as much warning as possible that redundancies would be necessary.

Changes to terms and conditions

Contractors want, if possible, to harmonise terms and conditions of employment. TUPE restricts their ability to do this in two ways. Firstly, it entitles employees to the same terms and conditions with the contractor that they had before the market test, unless they agree to accept a different package. Secondly, it prevents the contractor from unilaterally changing terms and conditions. This is because changes to terms and conditions which are not for an "economic, technical or organisational reason" are automatically unfair. The only practical means by which an employer can unilaterally impose changes on employees is by dismissing them and offering them re-employment on new terms. If the procedure is carefully handled and the new terms are justifiable in terms of the needs of the business, such dismissals should be fair. TUPE prevents this because dismissals which are simply to harmonise terms and conditions of employment will not be for an "economic, technical or organisational reason".

In practice contractors and the client organisation will normally overcome this problem by seeking agreement to the changes either before or after the transfer takes place. Before the transfer the employer is obliged to inform employees of measures which the contractor intends to take in relation to terms and conditions. It is therefore important to the marketing testing organisation to know what changes the contractor proposes to make. This point should be covered in the contract documentation.

Pensions

Both TUPE and the Directive exclude pension rights from the terms and conditions which transfer to the contractor. Article 3 of the Directive states that:

> "Rights to old-age invalidity or survivors' benefits under supplementary company or inter company pension schemes outside the statutory social security schemes are not transferred".

It is generally believed that the effect of this provision is to exclude rights under occupational pension schemes, whether those schemes are contracted in or contracted out. There is, however, some doubt whether contractors are entitled to impose significantly worse pension rights on employees who have been transferred under TUPE. Case law in this area is still developing but it is suggested that employees in this situation may be entitled to resign and claim constructive dismissal. Clearly, as with other changes to terms and conditions, the answer is to obtain agreement from the employees to substituting the new pension scheme for the old one.

Government guidance on the relevance of TUPE to market testing of public services

William Waldegrave, the UK's Public Services Minister, issued guidance on the implications for market testing of TUPE in March 1993. The guidance sets out the circumstances in which the regulations are, and are not, likely to apply, and explains their effect where they do. As the Minister stated, they are not designed as a complete statement of the law and do not obviate the need for legal advice. The guidance, which constitutes a fairly cautious statement of the law, is set out below:

Guidance on the relevance of the Transfer of Undertaking (Protection of Employment) Regulations to market testing of public services

(Issued by the Cabinet Office, Crown copyright.
Reproduced with the permission of the Controller
or Her Majesty's Stationery Office.)

1. The Transfer of Undertakings (Protection of Employment) Regulations 1981 (TUPE) may apply to certain contracts for services undertaken by the private sector following the market testing of public services. This document sets out considerations relevant to identifying the applicability of TUPE, as well as guidance on the effects of TUPE. The document is for information only and should not be regarded as a complete statement of the law. Each individual case must be considered in detail on its facts. This guidance does not obviate the need for legal advice to be taken.

The scope of TUPE

2. The TUPE Regulations implement the 1977 European Community Acquired Rights Directive. Proposed changes to the Regulations under the Trade Union Reform and Employment Rights Bill now before Parliament (including a clarification of their application to undertakings which are not commercial ventures) are described in the Annex to this guidance. They are taken into account in the description of the working of the Regulations set out below.

3. The Regulations apply when an undertaking (whether or not a business or part of a business which is an economic entity capable of operating as a going concern and which retains its identity is transferred from one employer to another. The Regulations do not apply when the assets of a business are simply disposed of without its operation being continued by the new employer. Nor do they apply to transfers affected through share take-overs which do not involve a change of employer.

4. The European Court of Justice (ECJ) has identified a number of considerations relevant to determining whether a business has been

transferred as a going concern. The crucial point is whether an "economic entity" has been transferred and remains in existence performing the same or similar activities. Various judgements of the ECJ have established that the following factors have to be taken into account in making this assessment:

- the type of undertaking or business in question;

- whether or not the tangible assets of the business (e.g. buildings and moveable property) have been transferred;

- the value of the intangible assets of the business at the time of the transfer;

- whether the majority of employees are taken over by the new employer;

- whether the customers of the former business are transferred;

- the degree of similarity between the activities carried on before and after the transfer, and the length of any period during which those activities were suspended.

The Court has however made it clear that these are only individual factors within the overall assessment that has to be made, and cannot be considered in isolation.

5. In the recent *Rask* case, the ECJ made clear that the Acquired Rights Directive may apply where an undertaking enters into a contract with another undertaking to provide a service which had previously been managed directly. The judgement does not say that the Directive *must* apply in such situations and emphasises the need to consider whether an economic entity has been transferred (in the Rask case the contractor was required to take full operational responsibility for a canteen and to employ all the existing staff).

Application of the Regulations to contracting out

6. In relation to the contracting out of an area of work following market testing or compulsory competitive tendering, the question in each case is therefore whether the new arrangement involves a transfer of an undertaking, in the terms of the TUPE Regulations. On

21 January 1993, in a statement to the Commons Standing Committee on the Trade Union Reform and Employment Rights Bill, the Attorney General set out the principles regarding the "transfer of an undertaking" as follows:

> 'It is clear from the case law that under both the [EC Acquired Rights] Directive and the [TUPE] Regulations, [transfer of an undertaking] means the transfer of an economic entity which is capable of operating as a going concern and which retains its identity. The contracting out of a service is not a transfer of an undertaking unless it involves enough of the elements of the original operation such as premises, staff, goodwill or customer base to constitute the transfer of a going concern.
>
> "But no single one of these [elements] is essential for there to be a transfer. The case law makes clear that it is the overall sum of what is transferred which determines whether there has been a transfer of an undertaking".

7. This means, for example, that the fact that a majority, or even all, of the employees are re-employed by the new employer does not necessarily indicate a transfer of an undertaking for the purpose of the Regulations. Market testing is likely to lead to a range of new arrangements for carrying out activities currently within the public sector. In some circumstances the transfer of many elements of the original operation will be involved; in others few if any will be transferred. It is not possible to lay down hard and fast rules for determining whether or not the Regulations may apply to the contracting out of a particular operation as a result of market testing, or to provide a comprehensive list of the factors to be taken into account.

8. Some circumstances in which the Regulations are likely to apply are as follows:

- where the new employer employs substantially the same staff to do the same work as before, using the same premises and the same equipment for the work;

- where the new employer is unable to do the work without keeping on a group of key employees who can be regarded as an essential asset;

- where the new employer takes on substantially the same employees as recognisably the same organisational unit;

- where the former employer makes it a condition of the contract, or there is an understanding between the parties, that the new employer will continue to use the same employees for the same work (it is the Government's policy that public sector organisations that invite tenders for the performance of public services should not impose such conditions except for reasons strictly related to the performance of the service in question);

- where, whether or not any employees are taken on, the new employer takes over the management or control of premises, assets or equipment which

    (1)   were used by the previous employer to carry out the activity in question;

    (2)   are significant in relation to that activity; and

    (3)   are managed or controlled by the new employer for the purpose of carrying on that activity.

9.   In the Government's view the Regulations are unlikely to apply to instances of market testing:

- where the new employer conducts the operation substantially differently, without making significant use of previous staff, key employees, premises or equipment;

- where the identity of the previous undertaking is substantially changed and any staff taken on by the new employer are incorporated into a different organisational structure.

What the Regulations require

10. Where the Regulations do apply to a particular transaction, they place certain obligations upon the new employer concerning the contracts of employment of employees of the previous employer. The Regulations also lay down requirements concerning the dismissal of employees for reasons connected with the transfer, and the circumstances under which such dismissals will be regarded by the courts as unfair.

11. When the Regulations apply, the new employer takes over any collective agreement made on behalf of the employees which is in force immediately before transfer, and the recognition of any independent trade unions. However, the new employer will be in exactly the same position as the existing employer in deciding whether he wishes to continue to operate such collective agreements or trade union recognition after the transfer. The recognition of any independent trade union will lapse if the transferred business does not continue to have an identity distinct from the remainder of the new employer's business or if the new employer chooses not to recognise the trade union.

12. When the Regulations apply the new employer also takes over liability in respect of the contracts of employment of all employees who were employed by the previous employer immediateliy before the transfer and of any persons who would have been so employed if they had not been unfairly dismissed for a reason connected with the transfer. The new employer is bound by all the terms and conditions of the contracts of employment which are taken on, with the exception of criminal liabilities and employees' occupational pensions.

13. Dismissal connected with a transfer will be held to be unfair automatically unless the dismissal is necessary for an economic, technical or organisational reason (see below); the individual will have a remedy against the new employer. Under employment law, an employee has potential remedies for constructive dismissal and/or breach of contract when the employer unilaterally alters his overall terms and conditions of employment, including pensions, to his disadvantage. This also applies when an undertaking is transferred.

14. Only where the dismissal is necessary for an economic, technical or organisational reason entailing changes in the work force can the previous or new employer fairly dismiss an employee in the context of a transfer. The courts have tended towards a narrow interpretation of such reasons; for example the willingness of the new employer to charge less for providing a service if the old employer agreed to dismiss the existing work force would not qualify.

15. Examples of circumstances in which a dismissal might be regarded as fair are:

177

- where demand for an employer's output has fallen to such an extent that profitabiity could not be sustained unless staff were dismissed (economic reason);

- where an employer wishes to use new technology and the employees of the previous employer do not have the necessary skills (technical reason);

- where the new employer operates at a different location from the previous employer and it is not practical to relocate the staff (organisational reason).

In such cases dismissals will be fair provided that the employer has acted reasonably in the circumstances.

16. In such a situation, the employee concerned may be eligible for a redundancy payment. The previous employer will be liable for redundancy payments if the redundancy takes effect before the transfer. If the redundancy takes effect after the transfer, the new employer will be liable for redundancy payments including payments in respect of any continuous service with the previous employer. If they are not subsequently renegotiated, those payments must be on the same contractual terms as those in force before the transfer.

17. Where the Regulations apply the previous and new employers must inform and consult any independent recognised trade union about the transfer. The information must be provided sufficiently in advance of the transfer to give adequate time for consultation and must include:

- notification that the transfer will take place, its approximate timing, and the reasons;

- the legal, economic and social implications of the transfer for the affected employees;

- whether the employer intends to take any action which will affect the employees and, if so, what; and

- where the previous employer is required to give the information, the activities which the prospective new employer proposes to carry out.

18. The existing employer must consult the trade union representatives of his employees about action which will affect them whether or not they are employed in the undertaking (or part of it) to be transferred. During these consultations he must consider and respond to any representations made by the union representatives. If he rejects these representations, he must state the reasons.

ANNEX: Changes to TUPE in the Trade Union Reform and Employment Rights Bill 1992

1. As the Regulations currently stand, they exclude transfers of undertakings which are not 'in the nature of a commercial venture'. The Government has, however, proposed removing this restriction in the scope of the Regulations and a provision to that effect is contained in the Trade Union Reform and Employment Rights Bill which, subject to Parliamentary approval, is expected to come into force in late 1993 or early 1994.

2. This change is being made to bring the wording of their Regulations into line with that of the Acquired Rights Directive and to clarify its interpretation. It is, however, unlikely to have any significance in the market testing context. The fact that an activity was originally carried out by a Government Department without charge should not be taken as implying that the Regulations will not apply if the activity is subsequentliy contracted out. In practice, any undertaking which can be contracted out is already likely to be capable of being described as 'commercial in nature' and therefore within the scope of the Regulations. The real test of whether the Regulations will apply, as indicated in paragraph 3 of the guidance, is whether what is being contracted out retains its identity as a going concern. This test remains unchanged.

3. A further amendment in the Bill makes clear that it is not necessary for property to transfer to a new owner for there to be a transfer of an undertaking. The Bill also makes clear that consultatin with employee representatives must be in good faith, with a view to seeking agreement.

4. As promised in the Citizen's Charter White Paper, the Bill also amends the Regulations to remove the possibility that a civil servant transferred under them could be entitled to a redundancy payment

even though he was continuing to do the same job on the same terms and conditions as before. The amendment to the Regulations makes it clear that, where there is a relevant transfer, the general exclusion of occupational pension rights from the automatic transfer of rights does not extend to benefits paid from an occupational pension scheme which are not for old age, invalidity or survivors. It puts beyond doubt the current position, namely that civil servants' rights to redundancy compensation automatically transfer into the new employment, and that no redundancy compensation is payable where civil servants transfer under the Regulations.